Opening the Gifts of Christmas

Opening the Gifts of Christmas

Opening THE Gifts of Christmas

PRACTICING THE ANGELIC GIFTS OF FAITH, HOPE, CHARITY, *and* LOVE

JENNIFER BASYE SANDER
and JAMIE C. MILLER

**Andrews McMeel
Publishing**

Kansas City

05 06 07 08 09 FFG 10 9 8 7 6 5 4 3 2 1

ISBN-13: 978-0-7407-5490-6
ISBN-10: 0-7407-5490-4

Library of Congress Control Number: 2005047836

To Laura, our own Christmas angel

Contents

The Gift of Hope

The Gift of Charity

The Gift of Love

INTRODUCTION

"To perceive Christmas through its wrapping becomes more difficult with every year."

—E. B. White

I magine a world in which people were able to feel the warm, magical spirit of Christmas each day of the year. A world where we believed that each day was a special gift and where we treated our family and friends—even our casual acquaintances—as if they were gifts too. A world in which that special feeling of love and brotherhood continued long after the ornaments and wrapping paper were packed away and the lights were taken down.

"Oh, would that Christmas lasted the whole year through, as it ought," Charles Dickens lamented. "Would that the spirit of Christmas could live within our hearts every day of the year." Like Dickens, people for centuries have wistfully imagined this ideal. But can this state of mind and heart ever really be achieved? Is it possible to open the gift of Christmas and feel its wonder and magic all year long?

Yes, we really think it is. With the inspiration and insight revealed in the pages that follow, you will learn how to practice the hallmark virtues of the Christmas season—Faith, Hope, Charity, and Love—in small and simple ways, creating a little more of December's love and harmony throughout the year. We believe that by reflecting on these four virtues a little more often you will be more likely to view Christmas as a starting point. Like a glorious gift that sits on your hearth long after December, it will infuse the other months with great joy and personal peace.

Now, don't misunderstand. Our message is not that you should keep the tree and the lights up all year round, nor do we intend to detract from the special magic that permeates the air every December. To the contrary, there will always be something special and sacred about the Christmas season; an attempt to *create* Christmas every day of the year would not only be futile, it would make the real holiday seem ordinary. What we hope to do, instead, is simply help you internalize the spirit of Christmas so that you will feel a little of its magic—and its reassuring peace—more often during the year.

Why do we call Faith, Hope, Charity, and Love the four Christmas Virtues? According to tradition, these four Virtues exist as a choir of heavenly angels—the fifth choir of nine choirs of angels in the heavenly hierarchy that starts at the bottom with ordinary angels and reaches up to the Seraphim and Cherubim. It is believed by many that the Virtues are the very angels who accompanied Jesus on his journey to heaven and are sometimes described as divine beings who perform the will of God.

By putting these Christmas virtues to work in everyday moments, you too will be performing the will of God. The angelic choir of Virtues is the essence of goodness made manifest through acts of kindness here on earth. As we become the hands of heaven, we invite these angels to walk among us dressed as ordinary people—a brother, a friend, a co-worker, a grandmother, a stranger, a child—people we know, people we can help and be helped by in return.

The true stories in this book are meant to be enjoyed not only during the holiday season but also throughout the year. Instead of reading them only once during the warmth of the holidays, we hope you will return to them again and again whenever you feel your grasp on the four Virtues fading away. In addition, at the end of each story are suggestions of simple and practical ways to more consciously embrace each virtue throughout the year.

We hope that the messages herein will lift and inspire you, and help you more easily spread the Gift of Faith, believe in the Gift of Hope, practice the Gift of Charity, and accept the Gift of Love.

The Gift
of Faith

In New York City more than a century ago, Dr. Philip O'Hanlon came face-to-face with a minor family crisis. In 1897, his only child, eight-year-old Virginia, came to him with some confusion. She'd been talking to her friends, and what she heard from those friends worried her. Could her father help her out?

Virginia's confusion had to do with Santa Claus; it seems her friends had planted some doubts about his existence. So her father did what any father would do under the circumstances: he passed the buck. He suggested she write a letter to the newspaper instead—to the *New York Sun*.

"It was a habit in our family," Virginia said years later, "that whenever any doubts came up as to how to pronounce a word, or some question of historical fact was in doubt, we wrote to the Question and Answer column in the *Sun*. Father would always say, 'If you see it in the *Sun*, it's so,' and that settled the matter."

Her hand-scrawled letter found its way into the hands of a veteran editor, Francis P. Church, son of a Baptist minister. Church was a practical yet warmhearted man whose personal motto was "Endeavor to clear your mind of *can't*." When controversial subjects had to be tackled on the editorial page, especially those dealing with theology, the assignments were usually given to Church.

Now Church had in his hands a little girl's letter on a most controversial matter, and he was burdened with the responsibility of answering it: "Is there a Santa Claus?" He bristled when his boss first handed him the assignment, but he quickly realized there was no avoiding the question. He must answer, and he must answer truthfully. And so Francis Church got down to work and wrote his reply, which was to become one of the most memorable editorials in newspaper history.

> Yes, Virginia, there is a Santa Claus. He exists as certainly as love and generosity and devotion exist, and you know that they abound and give to your life its highest beauty and joy. Alas! how dreary would be the world if there were no Santa Claus! . . . There would be no childlike faith then, no poetry, no romance to make tolerable this existence. . . . The eternal light with which childhood fills the world would be extinguished.
>
> —*New York Sun*, September 21, 1897

Church's response was most likely intended for his adult readership as well as for the Virginias of the world. He reminds old and young alike to put cynicism aside and look at the world through the innocence of childhood, and that only through trust and faith can we see the true radiance and wonder of our existence. He insists that it is our willingness to believe in something intangible that makes Christmas—and life—worth celebrating.

Francis Church continues his letter to Virginia by underscoring his sentiments about belief and faith: "Nobody sees Santa Claus, but that is no sign that there is no Santa Claus. The most real things in the world are those that neither children nor men can see."

We celebrate Christmas today because of One who came into the world as a little child, and though He wore the mantle of divinity, He understood the childlike frailties and human longings in each of us. When we have a yearning—a feeling that something is missing in life—perhaps it is our soul yearning for its heartland, a longing to once again believe.

Just Sing

JOAN WESTER ANDERSON

"I believe that the eternal lesson of Christmas is to inspire us to use our God-given gifts to build a better world."

—Norman Vincent Peale

She should never have waited so long to tackle the Christmas shopping, Kimberley Little reminded herself as she shifted her bundles from one aching arm to the other. She hated shopping, hated having to brave the crowds and sift through endless piles of merchandise. But there was only so much holiday gift-buying one could do through catalogs, and of course the children needed their annual photo taken with Santa Claus. So here she was, imprisoned in a slow-moving "Visit Santa" line, wondering if she might spend the entire holidays in this Albuquerque mall.

She had to admit she was never "up" at this time of year, no matter how smoothly things went. Her father had died tragically in a plane crash just a few days before Christmas when Kimberley was fourteen, and although many years had passed she never faced December without feeling echoes of that familiar shock, sorrow, and loneliness. As her faith matured, Kimberley had gotten involved in her church, singing in the choir, teaching her young sons to pray. She didn't doubt that her father was in heaven with Jesus and that she would see him again someday. But every year as Christmas approached, the same nagging question emerged: If this is all supposed to be so wonderful, why don't I feel that way?

Juggling her packages again, Kimberley looked at her three young sons. Their moods seemed no cheerier than hers. One was demanding a ride on the train farther down the mall. Another was hungry. "I hate Christmas!" muttered the eldest, his lip thrust out in frustration.

Kimberley felt guilty. "Moms have so much influence on the spirit of the family," she thought. If we're just a little bit cranky, everyone picks up on it. She didn't want to spoil the season for the children—they shouldn't carry the same vague sadness that she did. And yet as she glanced around at the other families in line, she realized they were all like hers. The kids were irritable, tired, fighting with one another, the parents grimly determined to endure.

Why are we like this? Kimberley wondered. Where was the real Christmas, the spirit of love and peace, the joyful awareness that a Savior had come into the world? How did one cut through the confusion, the fatigue, the pressure—yes, even the bittersweet memories—to find it?

Suddenly, God nudged her. "It couldn't have been anything else," Kimberley recalls, "because all at once I felt a little tingle, as if something new was happening. And I realized that if I wanted to feel better about myself, I had to take the first step. I had to be brave." But how?

Sing a carol. The suggestion was already in her heart. She had recently performed a solo in church. She knew how to sing. But this noisy shopping center was not church. "Oh, no, God, not me," she told Him silently. "You remember how shy I am. People will stare."

Bring Christmas to the mall. Just sing.

Kimberley sighed. It was no use. She knew that voice. And hadn't she asked Him where Christmas was?

Softly she began to sing. "Silent night, holy night . . ." The couple in front of her, who had been filling out a photograph order form, paused and turned around.

"All is calm, all is bright . . ." Kimberley reached for her youngest son and picked him up. What if they threw her out of the mall for disturbing the peace?

"You're bringing peace," the answer came. "Sing."

The children behind her had stopped arguing. "Listen," one whispered to the other. "That lady's singing."

The tips of Kimberly's ears turned red. "Round yon' virgin, mother and child . . . ," she went on. Her sons would never speak to her again. But then—was it her imagination or did she hear another voice? And another? Yes, the couple in front of her were singing, their order form forgotten. Now the children behind her . . . and their parents . . . and the family next to them . . . singing *and* smiling. Dazed, Kimberley realized that the entire section of the Santa Claus line had joined her. Even her own children.

It was true! Little risks could lead to wonderful things. And she was feeling better—her spirit soothed, her mind quieted. Maybe Christmas and its eternal message was simply as close as anyone allowed it to be.

Voices faded as the song ended. "Let's do 'Angels We Have Heard on High,'" Kimberley suggested to the people around her. It was her oldest son's favorite carol, and her dad had always loved it too.

It was going to be a wonderful Christmas after all.

★

The sounds of hymns and carols do so much to put us in the holiday mood. Why not try to recapture the feeling at other times of the year too?

If you own a Nativity set, get it out in the spring— maybe around Easter, if that season has special significance for you. If a Nativity set isn't part of your Christmas, envision what the Holy Family might have looked like. While listening to Christmas music, take each piece in your hand and try to visualize the part that person or object played in the event more than two thousand years ago. Ponder the scene as if you were there at the time. Smell the fresh hay beneath your feet, listen to the lowing of the cattle and bleating of the sheep, picture the new, wrinkled skin of the tiny baby. Think about how the humble shepherds might have felt. What hopes and fears would be going through everyone's minds?

Over two thousand years ago, Christ's birth wasn't about busy malls and shopping lists, it was about simple acts of kindness, love, and worship. In the midst of a busy mall, Kimberley learned that something as simple as a song could restore everyone's spirits and connect a group of strangers. Ask yourself how you can simplify your life now and at Christmastime to open up more room in your heart for the things that matter most.

The Carolers' Mystery

STEPHEN LAUDI

"For an hour on Christmas Eve and again on the Holy Day;
Seek the magic of past time, from this present turn away."

—Robinson Jeffers

Montreal used to be known as the "City of Churches." The role of the church in the city has declined somewhat over the years, but the influence can still be seen in the way that all of Montreal embraces the Christmas season. The efforts of residents, merchants, and city workers alike turn the city's wide boulevards into a glittering fantasyland ablaze with decorations and lights. And it was on one of those wide boulevards that our Christmas miracle occurred.

I was president of the community council for Notre Dame de Grâce that year. One of my duties involved organizing a large public caroling party. We wanted to involve not just church members but also as many people from the surrounding community as we could. Christmas is a wonderful time of year to reach out, and we hoped that our party, "A Christmas Caroling," would accomplish that. We invited many choir members (and anyone else who could carry a tune) and friends to join us one night on the sidewalk of Sherbrooke Street.

Sherbrooke Street is a wide downtown street lined with stately old elm trees. The heavy branches of the trees were gaily decorated with colored Christmas lights, which were reflected in turn on the dark, slick streets below. It was a magical look. The turnout was great: a group of thirty-five adults and children all bundled up against the snowy night, clutching songbooks in their gloved hands. A multitude of voices soon filled the air as we warmed up with some old Yuletide favorites: "Hark the Herald Angels Sing" and "The Twelve Days of Christmas." I was excited; this community event was everything I'd hoped for, with one small exception. It was *cold.*

Our plan was to stand on the sidewalk and sing for passersby instead of going door-to-door. As we assembled to begin, I noticed a few singers look longingly into the frosted windows of a restaurant behind us. The restaurant was pleased at the presence of such a large group of singers and had even offered to give us all free hot chocolate that evening. I decided that the time for hot chocolate had arrived.

The group of singers filed one by one down the eight narrow stairs that led into the small restaurant, grateful that a warm drink was on the way. We stood together in the center of the room, waiting for our group to reassemble at the tables. A small parade came slowly down the stairs. It took a few minutes before the last of our group stepped into the toasty restaurant. And then it happened.

No sooner did we all sit down than a loud crash rang out. We felt the building shake, and we rushed up the stairs toward the door. And there, at the very spot on the sidewalk where our large group of singers had stood just moments before, lay a large electric company truck, its broken wheels spinning. The driver of the Hydro-Québec truck had lost control on a patch of black ice as he drove down Sherbrooke Street and had crashed head-on into the street lamp.

We did sing our carols that night. Too shaken to stand out on the street again, we stayed in the warmth of the restaurant and sang for the truck driver, the police, and the owners of the restaurant, whose generous offer of hot chocolate had spared us all.

✫

Although some might call this incident a mere coincidence, the carolers who were there believed they had witnessed a true Christmas miracle.

It has been said that miracles are God's way of remaining anonymous, but the hands through which He works are clearly visible: the hands of ordinary people all around us. A simple act of kindness can be the miracle someone else is praying for—and all it takes is to keep our hearts and minds open to the whispers that nudge us in the direction of the needs of others.

One creative way of focusing on others throughout the year is to make an old-fashioned paper-chain out of strips of construction paper looped together. This is especially fun if there are children in your home—you can even make twenty-five loops to count down to Christmas if you make the chain in December.

Before you tape or glue the strips into circles, however, write the name of a family member, friend, or acquaintance on each strip. Each night when you remove a loop, read the person's name and focus for a few minutes on that person—their life, their gifts, their needs. Your positive energy in that person's behalf might spark the very miracle they need most in their life at the time.

A Special Request

FRANK BARANOWSKI

> *"Christmas Eve was a night of song that wrapped itself about you like a shawl. But it warmed more than your body. It warmed your heart—filled it, too—with a melody that would last forever."*

—Bess Streeter Aldrich

We were busy. With Christmas just a handful of days away, every talk-show host at the station was searching for the best in radio programming. After all, Christmas is a special time of year. To help create a meaningful and memorable radio show for all your listeners, you want the pageantry, the glory, and the mystique of the season. So you dig, hoping to find some little-known fact or new story to build on. But after nine years on the air in Phoenix, Arizona, with my show *Mysteries Around Us*, a program dealing with unexplained phenomena, I was scraping the bottom of the holiday barrel.

Coming from the Midwest as I do, it is easy to remember the sights and sounds of my childhood holidays: snow-draped Christmas trees, and caroling parties where the cold night air was filled with the sweet sound of German, Polish, and Italian carols. And the food. A good cook on any day, Mom outdid herself at holiday time. I have wonderful memories of holidays past, memories I treasure still.

"Perhaps I could re-create that same experience for my listeners," I thought, as I rummaged around for inspiration. I couldn't give anyone in Phoenix a snow-draped Christmas tree or cold night air, but the town does have a diverse ethnic mix; folks have moved here from all corners of the world. I could put together a program of stories and music from many countries in the hope that it might rekindle memories of another time, another place, for some of the listeners out there.

One of the songs I planned to use on the air was a traditional Polish carol: "Hush-a-Bye Wee Jesus." In Polish it's called "Lulajze Jezuniu." "Would I even be able to find a recording of that?" I wondered, as I drew up my dream list of songs I'd like to play. But luck was with me, and I found a CD recording by a Canadian group known as the Billy Andrusco Trio—and the CD had not one but two recordings of the song, one with the words in English and one in Polish. My playlist was complete, and I settled in to do the show.

That night, moments after I played "Hush-a-Bye" on the air, a call came in to our station's technical director. Would we please play the Polish version of the song again? And not just once, but over and over and over again?

I will admit that my first impulse was not in the spirit of giving—I wanted to shrug off the request. I'd put a lot of thought and effort into crafting this international musical tour. We had finished playing the music of Poland and were now well into the Christmas music of Germany. And not only that, but to play just the Polish version was impossible. You had to listen to the English version first.

But my moment of selfishness passed quickly, and I heard a quiet voice in my heart. "Do it!" the voice urged. "Go ahead and grant someone's Christmas wish. Do it now!" And so I did. I asked the director to fade out the German carols and slowly bring up "Hush-a-Bye." Not knowing the reason behind the odd request we'd received, I simply explained that the song meant a lot to me. Which is actually true—my mother used to sing it to me when I was a small child.

My technical director and I listened in astonishment to what happened next. Instead of hearing the English version of the carol that started the track, we heard the Polish version! It was technically impossible, but that was what we were hearing. As I was to learn later, that was not the only impossible thing that happened during that program.

Two days after the holiday music program aired I received a call from a young man who insisted on seeing me. "Not a chance," I replied. "It's too close to Christmas, and I'm too busy." He quickly changed my mind, though, when he told me he was the one who'd called to request repeated playings of "Hush-a-Bye" and that he had a story to share with me.

We met just a few hours later. He grasped my hand and shook it so hard and so long that I thought he'd never stop. His rapid speech was broken only by the tears that streamed down his face and the frequent blowing of his nose. This is his story:

His name is Walter, and he is of Polish descent. His mother, Clara, whom he loved dearly, had suffered a massive stroke that left her paralyzed and unconscious. She surprised the doctors by living ten days in that condition when the expert opinion was that death was only a few hours away. Walter and his wife had been by her bedside at the hospital, prepared for the end but praying for a miracle.

The night of my radio show, shortly after ten o'clock, the strains of a familiar carol drifted into her hospital room. The music annoyed Walter at first. His mother was dying, and who wants to hear Christmas carols at a time like that? "It must be coming from the room across the hall," he thought, shaking his head in annoyance. "Some people just have no consideration."

"Look, Walter," his wife said then, "look at your mother." Clara's head seemed to shake slightly. Her lips twitched. Thinking death had arrived, Walter ran to the nurses' station for help.

The nurse summoned a doctor, but by the time the doctor arrived Clara was as before. Silent and unmoving, comatose. The doctor had no explanation for the head movement or the twitching lips and left soon after reading the monitor.

It was Walter's wife who believed the music had something to do with Clara's slight response. "Call the station, Walter," she urged, "ask them to play that Polish song again." And Walter did. By the time he returned to the room after making the phone call, the music he'd requested was playing. As he watched with his wife and the nurse, all three were stunned as Clara—who had been paralyzed for ten days—moved her head a full three or four inches, her jaw and bottom lip trembling as if . . . as if she were trying to sing the song. Walter needed no coaching. Half crying, half singing, he stood at his mother's bedside and sang "Lulajze Jezuniu, lulajze lulai, a ty go matuniu u placzu u tulaj."

As Walter tells it, even in her eighties his mother had insisted on attending Midnight Mass every Christmas. And her main reason was to sing "Hush-a-Bye Wee Jesus," her favorite carol. She wanted to sing it to the baby Jesus, just as she had sung it every night to her baby Walter.

You can imagine what happened next. Within hours his mother was awake and singing with anyone who would join her. Clara left the hospital about a week later. As for the music—well, no one has really figured it out yet. Walter thought the music was coming from across the hall, but it couldn't have been. You see, there are no radios on that floor of the hospital, and no intercom system that pipes in music. Could it have been someone carrying a boom box down the hall? No, those radios aren't allowed there either. And if someone had been sneaking around with one, Walter or the nurse would have spotted them. And why would the person with the forbidden radio have stopped just outside Clara's room?

I suppose the mystery will never really be solved, and maybe the details aren't important anyway. For me, it's enough to believe that Somebody Upstairs with the power to override all the hospital rules understood how important music is to the healing process and just wanted to hear Clara sing "Hush-a-Bye Wee Jesus" to Him one more time.

★

Christmas wouldn't be Christmas without music. In fact, music plays an integral role in most of life's important events and milestones. Try to imagine a graduation without hearing "Pomp and Circumstance"; a birthday without "Happy Birthday to You"; a wedding without the "Wedding March";

the Fourth of July without "God Bless America." Music evokes emotion and takes us back to memories of childhood as almost nothing else can.

Most families listen to Christmas carols during the season, but the custom of Christmas caroling from door to door, once popular in Europe and in earlier America, has dropped off our holiday agenda. But nothing takes less preparation or forethought. No equipment is needed except, perhaps, a string of jingle bells, some scarves and mittens, and a few willing family members or friends.

Consider inviting two or three other families to join you as you walk through your neighborhood singing. Or go in cars to three or four homes where you know someone is living alone or might be in need of holiday cheer. Visit a convalescent home; the patients won't care if the singing is out of tune, and they'll love the attention. Return home to hot chocolate, donuts, and a warm fire. Singing is good for the soul, so no matter how you arrange it, Christmas caroling will provide the joyful note that your holiday celebration needs.

You don't need to go Christmas caroling all year long to connect with the power of song, of course. Convalescent homes welcome groups of singers and visitors anytime. Perhaps you can even learn a few tunes that will connect the residents with their youth.

The Miracle of the Mounties

W. LaMar Palmer

"Joy is the serious business of heaven."

—C. S. Lewis

I was a member of the Royal Canadian Mounted Police in the mid-1950s. For several years our division, head-quartered in Winnipeg, Manitoba, brought Christmas to needy families of the province. Months before Christmas, we began to gather, repair, and build all sorts of gifts for the children.

Members of the Force were asked to donate anything that could be renewed, and clothing and toys came in from detachments all over the province. Money and gifts came in from other people too.

Some of the men built wooden toys—sleighs, wagons, and wheelbarrows—from donated lumber; the ladies donated sewing and knitting. Lists of the needy were gathered from town offices, schools, and churches, and then the gifts were sent to detachment personnel for delivery.

In 1955, I was in charge of a detachment in the inter-lake area of Manitoba. We'd had heavy snow in November and December, and travel in some rural areas was quite difficult. But nonetheless, on December 24 we went around the area delivering gifts—clothing, toys, festive food, and turkeys.

We had little difficulty reaching most of the homes by police car, but the most difficult one we left for the last: a family living on a little-used bush road about four miles from town. The family consisted of the mother and four children, ranging in ages from one and a half to eight years old. There was no father. They had no telephone. I had one of the junior constables with me, and we drove to the store to inquire about the roads and the exact location of the home.

The storekeeper drew a map for us and said we would be able to drive about three miles north, but from there the family lived on a side road that had not been plowed out. And he was quite concerned because he had heard nothing from them for about two weeks. He gave us some candy and nuts to add to our gifts and asked us to report back to him with a list of things they needed.

By this time it was nearly seven o'clock, and dark. It was cold, but fortunately there was no wind. The sky was clear and there was a bit of a moon. We managed the three miles without difficulty, but at the side road our hearts sank. The road was filled with snow; there was not even a trail through it. We studied it carefully and wondered whether we should even try to walk. If only we had brought our snowshoes! We were about ready to turn back when my companion said, "It's going to be a bleak Christmas for those kids."

I agreed. "Let's give it a try," I said. "We can put the box of toys on the sled, one of us will pull while the other pushes, and we can balance the load on the sled."

We started out, but the snow was over our knees in most places, and it was hard going. Often we considered turning back. Besides, we could scarcely see, and we were afraid we would miss the house. The journey of only a little over half a mile seemed like a hundred miles. I guess thoughts of my own young children kept up my determination. Finally my companion thought he saw a light through the trees, and a short time later we saw a small cabin with a dim light in the window. We had found them!

Almost exhausted, we struggled through a gate in the wire fence and up a bit of path to the house. Inside we could hear children's voices. After we knocked, there was complete silence for a few moments, and then the door slowly opened.

It must have been a shock to them to see two burly policemen dressed in buffalo coats. They looked apprehensive, but when they saw the sleigh and box of presents, the expressions changed to amazement and joy. One little voice cried, "See, Mama, Santa Claus did come!"

The mother burst into tears. Then she threw her arms around us and kissed us soundly. "You are an answer to our prayers," she said. "It's a miracle—nothing else—just a miracle!"

Through her tears she told us she had tried to explain to the children that Santa would not be able to find them this year with all the snow, and that there wouldn't be any presents or any Christmas dinner. But the children wouldn't believe it. The oldest boy had said, "We can always pray," and he insisted that they all kneel together. Because the other children wanted to, the mother had agreed, but she dreaded the disappointment they would suffer when their prayers were not answered.

"We had hardly said 'Amen' when you wonderful men knocked on the door," she told us.

With joy in our hearts we laid out the big turkey and other food and gifts, and then we were smothered with hugs and kisses from four little children. Everyone shed tears of joy, including the two big policemen.

The family had not dared leave the home because of the deep snow. Although they still had flour and home-grown vegetables, they were getting low on other impor-tant items. Before we left, the mother gave us a list of things they needed most, and the children showered us with more hugs and a thousand "thank-you's." The trip from the car to the house had been a struggle every step of the way, but on the return journey we were so over-whelmed by the Christmas spirit that we just about floated back.

Christmas the next day with my wife and three little boys was made even more joyful by the memory of four little faces in a humble cottage way out there in the bush, and their faith in the spirit of Christmas.

★

Ah, the prayer of a little child—there is so much we can learn from them. Children aren't afraid to ask God for what they need. They are straightforward with Him, expressing wholehearted belief in His ability to bless and comfort them. They trust implicitly in His ability and power, and even when their prayer requests aren't "answered," children are not ashamed to try again.

Whether prayer is already a part of your life or not, try praying as a little child. Be specific in your prayers—that will help you achieve a deeper level of sincerity and concentration. Pray with the faith and hope of a child—with the belief that, with God on your side, miracles are possible. By acknowledging a higher power, we are reminded that someone else is in charge and are comforted in knowing that we can turn at least a portion of our problems and pain over to that power.

Group Gift

SUZAN DAVIS

"Blessed is the season which engages the whole world in a conspiracy of love."

—Hamilton Wright Mabi

I need a miracle," I said out loud as I pulled my sweatshirt over my head. I'd been feeling sorry for myself again—my mother had been gone for almost five years, but my heart was still heavy, especially when I thought about my two girls who would never get to know her the way I had.

"Give me a sign that Mom is here," I said as I looked at myself in the mirror and then heard the unspoken response of others. "She lives in your heart. She *is* with you."

Just between you and me, it's not the same.

"And throw in a dog if you wouldn't mind—and make it a big one."

I couldn't believe my self-serving prayers, but my kids' recent insistence on getting a dog was also getting me down. We'd researched different breeds for months, and the girls were set on a little pup you could take to the mall in your purse—like the one in *Legally Blonde* or some Paris Hilton Chihuahua look-alike. I finally announced that no dog smaller than an entrée would be permitted in our house, whose perimeter was already surrounded by coyotes day and night.

Still fretting, I walked into the kitchen, where the answering machine was blinking. The message was short: "Hi, it's Lila. Want a dog?"

Our neighbor Lila often found homes for stray pets, and now she had a four-month-old German shepherd she was trying to place—far from the pint-sized pocketstuffers Katelyn and Savannah had envisioned. But the girls and I took one look at the square black snout shadowed by huge, brown marble eyes and we were goners. We named the gigantic concoction of fur, face, and feet "Wolfie."

Wolfie revived our family. We'd been barely tolerating each other lately—the girls were busy exerting their preteen independence and hormones, while their "anticool" mom was trying desperately to hang on to any shred of "family togetherness" she could muster. Wolfie became the common bond that drew us all together again.

Our pup renewed my drooping spirits in other ways too. His devotion was unconditional—he followed me into every room and would wait for me, looking out the window for hours when I'd leave. Wolfie hated being without me so much that I'd even take him to the college where I taught English. Like some of the students, he never took notes and often slept in class, but for that he was quickly forgiven when he'd jump up and proudly walk me back to the car. He took care of me in ways that were paralleled only by the love I had felt from my mother as a young girl. In some ways, Wolfie was the sign I'd hoped for that my mother was still there.

As perfect as Wolfie was in filling the emotional needs of our family, his physical condition worried me. He was eating no more than a few bites of food every few days, so right after Thanksgiving I finally took him to the vet. After briefly looking him over, the vet announced, "This is a disaster. This dog has no hip sockets, and his back legs, free floating, are poking his colon and other organs as he grows bigger."

The doctor continued with sorrowful eyes that frightened us. "Every day you spend with him makes you feel better, but every day he lives makes him feel worse. He doesn't eat because he hurts."

Shortly after receiving the depressing news about our dog, my friend Renelle called out of the blue. We hadn't talked in ages, but she intuitively knew something was wrong. You see, Renelle claims to be spiritually connected to animals, something I had given her considerable grief about through the years. As I explained our dilemma, Wolfie's head rested in my lap, his eyes fixed on me with such love that it made my heart melt.

Her words were startling. "God speaks to us through animals," she said. "Put him down—he'll thank you for it. He has done his job. He's mended your hearts, and he'll send you another in an unbroken body. Just wait and see." The torment and guilt inside me instantly dissolved.

Ten days before Christmas, Wolfie died. As devastating as it was, Renelle had infused in me an inexplicable sense of faith about the future.

A few days later my phone rang, and when I picked it up I heard the voice of my friend Dana shouting, "I've got your dog!" My stomach dropped for a split second before reality set in. She's made a mistake. She didn't know what had happened to Wolfie.

But before I could argue or explain, Dana continued, out of breath. "He was on Auburn-Folsom Boulevard with two lanes of cars flying by him in each direction. He was in an absolute panic, spinning in circles in the middle turn lane. I've got him in the car, and we're bringing him to your house." Dana Swain, the local Girl Scout leader, had done yet another good deed. No wonder I called her "The Amazing Swain," I would explain as soon as she arrived.

Several minutes later, a wet, muddy four-month-old German shepherd stood on our front porch under the light. The girls and I were stunned, our hearts pounding in unison.

"Is this what it's like to be in the Twilight Zone?" asked eleven-year-old Savannah.

It was like a reunion—as if a dear old friend was back. The children fell all over him—we all did. Dana hadn't known that Wolfie was gone, and the pup bore such an uncanny resemblance in size, weight, and demeanor that she had assumed it was he. After an exhilarating few hours our hearts grew heavy, knowing we'd have to check the Lost Pet section of the next morning's paper.

The dreaded call came at seven o'clock the next morning. Dana had seen a sign: LOST 4-MONTH-OLD GERMAN SHEPHERD. She gave us the phone number. As I reluctantly turned to make the call, I recalled a brief visit I'd had with a woman at a recent Christmas party. Our conversation had centered on our mutual losses—her lab had been recently killed along Auburn-Folsom Boulevard, and mine had recently been put down. When she mentioned wanting to buy a new pup for Christmas, I'd recommended that she consider a German shepherd. With phone book in hand, I felt compelled to look her name up. There it was—Marilyn Keithley. Her phone number matched the one on the Lost Dog sign.

Our brief and joyful encounter with the loving pup we called Maxx was replaced by deep sadness as we prepared to say good-bye to him. Savannah cried nonstop. "I've spent my whole life saving up nine hundred and ten dollars, and I'll give it all to the owner if she'll let us keep the dog. Please ask, Mom," she begged.

Marilyn Keithley flew through our front door, hugging and thanking us profusely. Tears streamed down her cheeks as she got down and hugged the pup to her chest. But after a minute or two, the dog gently meandered away from her and plopped down, his hind legs on one child and his head on the other. Marilyn sat back and silently took it in.

"God speaks to us through animals," she quietly announced, and then, after a long pause, said: "I don't know why I bought this dog. He wasn't really what I wanted, but I felt compelled to bring him home. I only had him an hour before he disappeared from the back-yard—through a fence that has held dogs for five years without an escape."

Marilyn paused again as we sat in stunned silence, breathless, afraid to make a move. Tears filled her eyes as she said firmly, "This dog has found his family. *You* are his family. It's not about me, and it's not about you. God has chosen you for him, and him for you. Some way, somehow, he found you."

A woman who hardly knew us but who intimately knew loss sacrificed the companion she had spent months searching for. The girls and I visited her home later that night. She sat alone on a long couch reading a book about dogs. An empty dog bed sat in the back of the room, but she assured us it would be occupied soon.

Today, Maxx lives happily with our grateful family. We overlook little things like chewed pajamas, disappear-ing slippers, and stuffed bears without stuffing—or noses.

We're reminded that we are taking life too seriously every time underwear magically reappears—plopped in plain sight like a special prize—just at the moment company drops in.

And each December my faith is renewed as I think about all those who took part in delivering a very special Christmas gift to our family—Lila, Dana, Renelle, Marilyn . . . my mother . . . and God, who indeed speaks to us through animals.

★

A kind woman sacrificed the companion she had spent months searching for—a personal sacrifice born out of love. Because she believed her actions were being directed from above, it was also an act of great faith.

Read "The Gift of the Magi" by O. Henry during a month other than December. Reflect on the concept of "sacrifice" and how it relates to love. What does sacrifice do for love? Is it the reason that mothers love their babies and children so much—because of the great personal sacrifice of caring for a dependent person?

Think of the last time you sacrificed something for someone else, and how you felt about it. If it's been a long time, think of a way you can be charitable to someone through a sacrifice of your time, your talents, or your resources, and then put your plan into action. Write it down. It might be as simple as going to a convalescent home and reading to an elderly person you don't know; it might be deciding to give a portion of your income to a charitable organization; maybe it's leaving work early to coach your son's T-ball game . . . But any form of loving sacrifice is good for the soul.

Blind Faith

SUZANNE PEPPERS

"To one who has faith, no explanation is necessary.
To one without faith, no explanation is possible."

—St. Thomas Aquinas

As the food was being passed around our Thanksgiving dinner table, each family member found a small card next to their plate. I had come across some preprinted Bible verses and thought they might get us all talking about our many blessings over the past year.

"Do you mind if I share my own verse?" my nephew Ryan asked. At age twenty-five, Ryan was true to form. In our conservative little family, his pierced ears, Fu Manchu beard, and rather bizarre style of dress made him stand out. But despite his looks, Ryan was a devout Christian and spent much of his time reading the Bible.

"I found a verse during my devotional time, Aunt Sue. I'd like to read that one, if it's okay with you. It's from Isaiah, chapter 55."

As Ryan leafed through the thin pages of his Bible, I thought about the contradiction before me. He'd been only thirteen when his parents divorced, a time that made him feel lost and alone in an upside-down world. Now Ryan was a young man struggling to grow out of his rebellious ways, clinging more and more to the traditional values of family, home, and faith.

"This verse means a lot to me because of something that happened this week, something that made me realize that I'm not really in charge of my life." And then he read, "As the heavens are higher than the earth, so are my ways higher than your ways, and my thoughts than your thoughts."

Ryan lowered his Bible, turned toward his fiancée, and took her hand. "Now that Jen and I are engaged, my new job as manager at the auto-lube shop is a real blessing. But the other day, things didn't look so bright. I was trying to remove some old fluid underneath a car but couldn't get the valve to open. Because my safety goggles kept fogging up, I took them off. Just then, the valve came loose and the fluid spilled right into my eyes and totally blinded me. Everything went dark. And all I could think of was that verse: ". . . My ways are higher than your ways, and my thoughts than your thoughts." I remember thinking, "Okay, God, I'm not sure what you have in mind for me as a blind person, but you must have something interesting up your sleeve."

Ryan went on to say that the fast thinking of the employees who quickly rinsed out his eyes and got him to the hospital for further treatment likely saved his sight. But the experience made him realize that in one moment the whole direction of any of our lives could change dramatically. Then he challenged us: "Are we all ready to accept change in our lives?"

The next night, my husband and I joined Ryan's mom and stepdad, Cyndee and Phil, to walk along Main Street for the Festival of Lights, a magical celebration that marks the beginning of the Christmas season. It was a scene out of a holiday movie, with a huge Christmas tree lighting up on cue, music and caroling, and the sweet sights, sounds, and smells of Christmas all around us. No one wanted the evening to end, but we finally said our "good-byes" and headed for home.

We hadn't been home more than ten minutes when the phone rang. It was Phil, and he was panicky. He told us that he and Cyndee had passed an accident on the way home—a truck that had gone off the road. The truck was Ryan's.

"They took him by helicopter, Sue. Dear God, let him be okay." He could hardly catch his breath.

A former police officer, Phil knew better than to stop at the scene of the accident when he had the victim's mother in the car. He had taken Cyndee home and then returned to the bridge where the white pickup was being pulled from the ditch.

"What happened here?" he asked the officer.

"Looks like a head injury. He went off the road, hit that tree, and then flew down the embankment. It looks pretty grim."

When we finally arrived at the hospital, Ryan's brother was already there. Cyndee ran from the car and collapsed into his arms. We made our way inside and were ushered into a family conference room, where Ryan's father, his siblings, cousins, and even some very close friends—seventeen in all—gathered in a tight huddle. It had been years since we'd seen Ryan's father, Steve; the divorce had not been amicable, and the relationships were more than strained.

An eternity later, the doctor arrived to give us the news. The medical diagnosis seemed like bullet points on a business presentation. The list sounded surreal: brainstem injury, coma, bleeding in both right and left ventricles, possible paralysis, certain brain damage, hooked up to a ventilator, possible tracheotomy—he'd be lucky to live through the night.

How could this be happening? Yesterday we were all gathered around the Thanksgiving table, expressing gratitude for blessings and talking joyfully about wedding plans and new jobs. But now we needed to focus on Ryan's life and on all we could do to save it.

"Let's pray." My husband, Cliff, gets calmer in a crisis. As a sheriff's lieutenant, he'd assisted at many accident scenes, but never at one that involved a family member, and I was touched by his sensitivity now. We all joined hands or held one another as we turned Ryan's condition over to God.

"A Bible! We need a Bible." My words broke the silence. "Remember? Ryan read to us from the Old Testament last night. Do you remember the verse? Does anyone remember? It was *his* verse—he claimed it. We need to read it to him now."

"Good idea. It was Isaiah 55," Cliff chimed in.

We ran to the chapel but could find only New Testaments. We jumped into the car and drove a block to the nearest hotel and explained our need to the man at the desk—who gave us a Bible from a nearby room. "Please keep it," the clerk insisted, no doubt seeing the desperation and grief in our eyes.

Back in the family waiting room, Ryan's sister began reading the verse he had shared the night before. It had been years since she'd opened a Bible, but tonight she read with tears in her eyes, begging for her brother's life to be spared.

Cliff and I entered Ryan's room together and were totally unprepared for what we saw. IV's, a ventilator, hands tied to the bed rails, a pressure monitor attached to his skull to measure the swelling in his brain.

"Ryan, honey, can you hear me? It's Aunt Sue." We touched him and told him we loved him. And then we weren't sure what else to say, so I opened the Bible to Isaiah 55 and began to read. As I did, Ryan's vital signs began to stabilize. It was incredible. The monitors indicated that his blood pressure was beginning to go down, as was the pressure in his head. Ryan was hearing us, and God was healing him—we were sure of it.

When we returned to the rest of the family, everyone sat stunned and silent. But within minutes Ryan's estranged parents were talking quietly together, discussing their son's life—almost parenting again, it seemed. By the end of the night, Cyndee and Steve were standing together over their son's bed, praying out loud for him.

Ryan was in a coma for just over three weeks—we were told that his awakening would be slow but steady. Most of us visited every day. We posted photographs of the family, of Ryan's life, of his fiancée, so that when he woke up he would remember. We prayed with him daily. We prayed with one another daily as we held each other up. I kept a book of all the cards and letters that came in, a record of all those who gave selflessly during those weeks and of the many blessings that came from this near tragedy. Steve's employer paid for a hotel for the family to stay in for two weeks, and scores of people brought food to help us get through the difficult days.

And then it happened. Just a few days before Christmas, Ryan suddenly sat up, opened his eyes, and said, "I'm okay!" Both his parents were there to hear those sweet words, and both recognized the moment as the most wonderful Christmas gift they would ever receive. Over the next few months, Ryan's functioning slowly returned. Therapy gave him back the use of his arms and legs, and he began to speak clearly after about six weeks. He had no recollection of the accident or of the time in the coma.

The e-mail updates I had sent family and friends, along with other cards and letters, became a book I called *While You Were Sleeping*. Ryan eventually read it and learned of the healing that took place in the world around him as his own body healed. A family divided by divorce was brought together again. A sister who had turned her back on God found renewed faith. Many of us who had been wrapped up in our own problems put them aside to love a young man back to health. And Ryan knew his family loved and cherished him; if there was ever a time he felt different or disconnected from them, those days were gone.

At Thanksgiving, Ryan had told us about his near brush with blindness during the accident at the auto shop. He enlightened us with the verse "My ways are higher than your ways, my thoughts than your thoughts" and stated that if God needed a blind man to do his bidding, Ryan would accept that challenge.

Ryan's head injury has left him legally blind, and now, just over a year since the accident, Ryan knows that God was preparing him for this moment. He was given that Bible verse. The first accident was a rehearsal, a test, and Ryan was faithful in responding to God with "I will trust you no matter what."

Without a doubt, that Christmas was the most significant and glorious season any of us had ever experienced. As we encircled Ryan's bed with love and prayers, we could feel the light of his faith—and the brightness of our hope—dispel the darkness.

★

Sometimes it can be hard to start a deep and thoughtful conversation, and giving a prompt can help. Suzanne encouraged her family to open up and talk about their blessings by handing out printed Bible verses, and her nephew Ryan shared his thoughts easily when discussing a verse he found meaningful.

Set aside one or two nights a month in which you and your family and friends get the conversation started with a favorite inspirational quote or literary passage, a Bible verse, or even a topical news story. By the time the holidays roll around again, you will all be able to talk openly about blessings and challenges you have experienced.

The Camel Had Wandered

JANET EYESTONE BUCK

"It comes every year and will go on forever. And along with Christmas belong the keepsakes and the customs. Those humble, everyday things a mother clings to, and ponders, like Mary in the secret spaces of her heart."

—Marjorie Holmes

I opened the box of Christmas decorations with child-like anticipation. Every year the items were the same, but after being carefully tucked away for eleven months it was like unearthing hidden treasures for the first time.

My fingers finally uncovered some of my favorite pieces: the Nativity set. My family had always enjoyed the Christmas tradition of setting out a ceramic Nativity scene—complete with wise men, camels, shepherds, sheep, and of course Mary, Joseph, and the baby Jesus.

And each season the Nativity scene was set out in the same artistic and elegant way.

I carefully unwrapped each piece, noticing once again the intricate details of the wise men's gifts, the curly wool of the sheep, the expression on Mary's face. I tenderly placed each figure, creating a display to represent that first Christmas, just how I imagined it might have been. My young children gathered around to watch. We talked about the birth of Jesus and the visit of the shepherds and the Magi. Then I cautioned the children, as always, not to touch the pieces, explaining that they were fragile and easily broken.

This year, however, the temptation was too great for my two-year-old daughter, Elizabeth. The day we set up the Nativity scene, I noticed several times, with some irritation, that a camel had wandered from its appointed place, or a sheep had strayed from the watchful care of the shepherd. Each time, I returned the piece to its rightful place, then tracked down the culprit and admonished her to leave things alone.

The next morning, Elizabeth awoke and went downstairs before I did. When I walked into the living room, I noticed right away that the manger scene had been disturbed again. All the pieces were clumped together in a mass, as tightly as they could be fit together.

I stepped forward impatiently to put things right, but I stopped short as I realized that some thought had gone into this new arrangement. All twenty-three figures were grouped in a circle, facing inward, pushed together as if pushing forward to get the best view possible of the figure resting in the center of them all, the baby Jesus.

My heart was touched as I pondered the insight of a two-year-old. Certainly, Jesus Christ should be the center of our holiday celebrations. If only we all could draw in together around the Savior, not only during the Christmas season but also during each day, we would have such a better perspective. The love He offers to each of us would be easily shared with others who have not ventured so close.

I left the Nativity arranged according to Elizabeth's design that year. During the rest of the season, it served as a poignant reminder of what Christmas is all about.

★

"And a little child shall lead them . . ." the Bible says. Like the family in this story, we have all learned valuable lessons because of the perceptiveness of a child.

Simple traditions like setting up a Nativity scene can provide wonderful opportunities for family togetherness and discussion. Another meaningful tradition is to read the story of the first Christmas together from the Bible. Many families do this every Christmas Eve, but it can be done anytime. Expose your family to the richness of the word of scripture. If you have young children, let them dress up in robes and towels and act out the story as Mom and Dad read it from the

*Bible (Luke 2 contains the most commonly used verses).
Invite extended family or friends over to participate and to
play the parts of shepherds, angels, and wise men. The experience will be enriching and faith-building and can be a lot
of fun too.*

He Came Home on Christmas Morning

MARGARET H. SCANLON

"No winter lasts forever; no spring skips its turn."
—Hal Borland

I was facing Christmas alone for the third time. It had been three years since my beloved husband passed away; he and I loved the holidays, and I had tried hard on my own to continue our traditions. I put up a real tree, built the little village underneath it, and put the tiny train together. I baked all the family specialties and invited the children over for Christmas dinner—but it wasn't the same. It never is.

We raised a large family together—three girls and five boys. And those eight children have now given me fifteen grandchildren. So it's a large crowd that gathers at my house every year for the holidays, and they all miss Papa's presence as much as I do.

That year, as usual, I attended Midnight Mass at our parish church. The Mass was, in fact, dedicated to my late husband, a bittersweet tribute and one that made me feel his absence all the more. Sitting in the smooth wooden pew, I let the music of the carols and the words of the sermon wash over me as my thoughts wandered back over my years with my husband, Dan.

We had always called Dan "the quiet man," for he was a man more given to gestures than to words. And his gestures over the years had been memorable: a bouquet of flowers for no particular reason; small gifts that would appear silently at my breakfast table. My favorite surprise was the evening he came up behind me and slipped a small diamond necklace around my neck. "Just a little something to make up for the bad times," he said as he fastened it in place. Oh, he could make me smile, that husband of mine.

The first Christmas without him was the hardest—at least until he made me smile. As I drove home from church that day, consumed by my new loss, I decided that a little Christmas music might distract me. I punched the button on the radio and settled back, expecting to hear "Silent Night" or "Angels We Have Heard on High," the typical Christmas Day fare. But what came over the airwaves was Andy Williams's soft rendition of "Danny Boy"—a strange selection for Christmas Day, I thought. It was a cheer-up gesture from Dan, I'm certain of it. And I knew he was still with me.

After Midnight Mass, I went home to my gaily decorated but empty house and settled in comfortably by a cozy fire. One by one I read the lovely holiday cards and messages that I'd received. Instead of the sadness I'd felt on previous Christmases, I had a feeling of peace. Before turning in that night, I quietly thanked God for all forty-six years that Dan and I had together.

Christmas morning dawned, and I set about preparing the house for the children and grandkids. My first task was to clean out the fireplace and lay a fresh fire. This had always been Dan's favorite job; he took particular care to build a long-lasting fire, with the logs and the kindling placed just so. I tried to take the same care, scraping out the burned chunk of wood from my fire the night before and sweeping out the ashes before setting the wood and kindling inside. I would wait to light it until the whole family was there.

My daughter Ginny was the first to appear. She cooked up a sumptuous breakfast as I put our holiday ham in the oven. Then we sat down together to share the early-morning feast.

"Gee, Ma, that's a great fire you built," Ginny said suddenly.

"Fire? What fire?" I asked. "I haven't started it yet. It's for later this afternoon."

"Well, turn around and look," Ginny urged. When I turned, I saw a beautiful fire blazing in my fireplace, a fire that I hadn't struck a match to. It was unmistakably one of Dan's fires.

My daughter and I sat together in the kitchen, marveling at the scene before us. Once again, it seemed that "the quiet man" was watching out for us, showing us with one of his small but tender gestures that he was nearby and thinking of us.

The warmth of the fire that year helped to melt away a little of the heartache my family still felt about our loss. For now we knew that, as lonely as we were without him, Dan was trying to let us know that we were still in his heart.

★

The natural cycle of life forces each of us to eventually deal with sickness, death, and loss of some kind, and the holidays are especially difficult for someone who has lost a loved one.

There are many simple things you can do to comfort the lonely at any time of the year. The word "comfort" comes from two Latin words: "com" and "fortis," meaning, "strengthened by being with." Be there. Run errands, help with normal routine chores, provide child care, offer to help get out Christmas ornaments and decorate their tree, invite them to Sunday dinner, Easter brunch, and summer picnics.

Instead of saying "Call if you need anything," simply do something—anything—to let that person know you care. Buy cards and help address, stamp, and mail thank-you notes to those who send flowers to the funeral; send a card or flowers on the one-year anniversary of the death. Being there to supplant empty hearts and lives with love and generosity during hard times is indeed part of the magic of Christmas.

The Gift
of Hope

After writing *Oliver Twist, The Pickwick Papers,* and *Nicholas Nickelby,* Charles Dickens thought he was at the peak of his career. But during the summer of 1843 his publisher informed him that sales were drooping and that it might be necessary to sharply reduce Dickens's monthly advances. The author was stunned and deflated. With four children, one more on the way, and his father and brothers begging for loans, Dickens became deeply troubled over his mounting debts.

His worries made it difficult for him to sleep, and Dickens spent many nights walking through the streets of London, searching for an idea that would earn him a large sum of money. From his home, he gradually neared the Thames River, where instead of the wealthy, elegant ladies and gentlemen of his neighborhood there were beggars, pickpockets, and bawdy streetwalkers. The dismal scene of tenement houses, litter-strewn streets, and open sewers reminded him of his own boyhood, the years when Charles worked twelve hours a day in a rat-infested warehouse in order to survive while his father lay in debtors prison. Now Dickens was tormented by the fear of not being able to pay his own debts.

As he started for home from his nightly walk one evening in late October, Dickens was feeling hopeless. His creativity and imagination were clouded by his depression, and he was no closer to the book idea that would save him financially than he was a month earlier.

But as he neared home on this particular night, he felt a sudden flash of inspiration. It was something he had never considered before, a Christmas story! Yes, a story written for the very people he passed on the streets of London, people who struggled with the same fears and longings he had known, people who hungered for just a bit of cheer in their dreary, difficult lives.

As the humid days of October turned to a cool November, the manuscript took form and the story took life. Each morning, Dickens was excited and impatient to begin the day's work. *A Christmas Carol* became a labor of love. It captured his own heart and soul, and he found himself weeping over and over again as he wrote. The manuscript was finished on December 2 and published just two weeks later.

Although Dickens would write many other finan-cially lucrative books—*Great Expectations, David Copper-field, A Tale of Two Cities*—none ever gave him the soul-satisfying joy he derived from his little Christmas tale. Eventually, some would call him the "Apostle of Christmas," and when he died in 1870 a poor child in London was heard saying, "Dickens dead? Then will Father Christmas die too?"

Like Dickens, people often do their best work in the midst of self-doubt and despair. From the storm of tribu-lation comes a gift, and when we acknowledge that gift our hope is once again restored. Despite discouraging cir-cumstances, disappointments, failures, and adversity, there is so much good within the limits of this life, and so much reason for faith in the future. The spirit of Christmas is in itself one piece of evidence of a brighter future, one that gives us a glimpse of hope—and almost, it seems, a glimpse of heaven.

But how do we keep hope in our hearts through all the seasons of our lives, even during our darkest days? Dickens's character, Scrooge, became known for keeping the Christmas spirit all year long, but we somehow miss the message that his incessant joy was made possible only after he had been redeemed and changed by his encounters. His is a story of rebirth, of new perspectives about people and priorities, of the possibility that comes from new beginnings.

Because Christmas falls at the end of the calendar year, most people consider the season to be a culmination, an end. But in other nations and cultures, Christmas Day marks the beginning of a period of worship, the beginning of a celebration that spills over into the new year. Indeed, if you stop to think about it, a story about a birth *is* a story of beginnings.

The Christmas story is about God giving each of us a fresh start, a chance at a new beginning. Many of our favorite symbols of the season reflect the promise of starting over. The evergreen Christmas tree, growing and greening through all the seasons of death in the natural world, embodies the promise that for every death there will be a rebirth; for every loss, a finding again; for every parting, a reuniting. The star atop the tree reminds us that even in the deepest darkness there is light, that for every seeker there is always a glimmer of hope.

When we allow the story to bring about new life in each of us, we will finally be able to keep the spirit of Christmas—the spirit of hope—alive in our hearts all year long.

All Alone for Christmas

BARBARA JEAN JONES

"Maybe Christmas," he thought, "doesn't come from a store.
Maybe Christmas—perhaps—means a little bit more."

—Dr. Seuss

Squinting at the bright winter sky, I was sure we were going to have a mild, sunny Christmas that year. That was somewhat of a disappointment, as I had come to love the snowy Christmases of Colorado. My thoughts were suddenly interrupted by an icy snowball splatting against my neck.

"Ha, ha! Gotcha!" screamed my little brother as he scurried away from me. It was the day before Christmas. At age thirteen, I was old enough to be left in charge of the house while our parents went into town ten miles away to pick up previously purchased Christmas gifts. So that we wouldn't prematurely discover our presents, Mom and Dad had cleverly arranged to leave them at the stores until Christmas Eve.

Trying to make the time go faster on what always seemed like the longest day of the year, my three younger brothers and I were playing in the three-day-old, crusted snow. We had started out making a snowman, but before long we were in a wild snowball fight.

"Ha, ha, ha! Gotcha back!" I yelled as I tackled my brother and the two of us fell, laughing, into a snowbank.

Although our family had moved to Denver more than six years before, it was still surprising to me how quickly the Colorado weather could change. Before our snowball fight had ended, the sky became overcast and, minutes after that, snow began to pelt the ground in furious streaks of gray.

Remembering that my parents had left me in charge, I gathered my brothers into the house and we spent the rest of the afternoon peering out at the driving snow, so thick now that the houses across the street were only dim shadows. The blanket of snow reached two feet, but still the heavy flakes continued to fall. I tried to sound confident as I told my brothers that our parents must be on their way home.

As evening drew near, one little brother playfully jumped off the front porch into the new snow. Were we ever surprised when all three feet of him disappeared into the snowy white! He reappeared looking like Frosty the Snowman.

Now it was early evening, and I was beginning to feel as grim as the quickly blackening sky. No parents. No phone call. Four frightened children alone in a storm on Christmas Eve.

Finally the phone rang. My heart beat rapidly as I answered. "Hello?"

It was my mother. My spirits rose, but quickly sank again when she told me what had happened. Mom and Dad were completing their errands when the blizzard had struck, coming on so suddenly and with such force that driving became impossible. Drivers had left their cars in the roads and walked to whatever shelter they could find.

After trying to get home all afternoon, our parents finally gave up, left the Christmas gifts in the car, and forged through the waist-deep snow toward the house of some friends. Mom was calling from their home.

I could feel her sadness and worry as she told me they wouldn't be able to make it home for Christmas. "Listen, honey, you've got to take care of your brothers and do whatever you can to make it a happy Christmas. We don't know when we'll be able to get back home."

Although I was relieved my parents were safe, my heart was heavy as I hung up the phone. "Some Christmas!" I said to myself. "How could I possibly make it happy?"

My younger brothers still believed in Santa. What was I supposed to tell them? There would be no Santa, no presents, and worst of all, no parents.

I could hardly look at my brothers' dismayed faces when I told them we'd be all alone for Christmas. But when my youngest brother started to cry, I made up my mind that somehow Christmas was still going to happen.

"Hey, guys, this'll be great," I exclaimed with hope. "We can stay up as late as we want and do something fun and different tonight."

The boys' moods began to brighten. We decided to gather our sleeping bags together and spend the night underneath the Christmas tree.

Pajama-clad, we gathered in the family room, cozied up in sleeping bags, gulped hot chocolate, and read the entire Christmas story from Luke. "Fear not, for, behold, I bring you good tidings of great joy" (Luke 2:10). I tried to picture the little baby Jesus on that cold night long ago, and I told my brothers that even though there were no presents or parties on that first Christmas, there was love and peace and happiness. I repeated the words "Fear not" over and over to myself, because I knew that I had to set the example of bravery for my younger siblings.

In spite of having no presents, no Christmas Eve party, no Santa, and not even parents, something magical happened that night. We felt the peace and comfort of knowing that Jesus Christ had come into this world to be our Savior. We felt this joy, this warmth, a feeling of love for our Savior and for one another—and that was all we needed. Looking back, it was one of the happiest Christmas Eves I can remember, that night when four children discovered the true joy of Christmas.

In the morning we awoke to weather that all but betrayed the storm of the previous day. All we could see was the warm light of the sun dancing off a frozen sea of snow. It was the loveliest Christmas morning I had ever seen.

As I sat enjoying the incredible scene, I was surprised to see two large objects racing toward our house. "It's Santa's sleigh!" exclaimed my youngest brother, amazed to see anything traversing this kind of snow. But the two snowmobiles that soon pulled up in our front yard brought something far better than Santa and his sleigh could possibly have brought us.

We ran to the door to greet two very relieved and joyous parents. Mom and Dad gathered us in their arms and hugged us tight. They explained that our neighbors, hearing of our plight, had given up their Christmas morning to make the long trip on their snowmobiles to bring our family together for Christmas. With tears running down their faces, they told us how happy they were to be safely home with us again and how proud they were of our courage.

Later, as we sat down to Christmas dinner, I marveled at the laughter and the chatting—it seemed that we couldn't get enough of being close together. We all felt true joy, even without the pile of gifts to unwrap or new toys and games to play with.

But as I looked around the table at the jubilant faces of my family, I realized that, even as a child, one doesn't need presents, parties, or Santa to feel joy at Christmas. The remarkable joy of Christmas comes from gifts money cannot buy: the companionship of loved ones, the warmth of the Christmas spirit, and most important, the gift of the Son of God.

✭

Four small children alone on Christmas Eve, their parents stranded and unable to come home. But through it all, Barbara and her brothers never gave up hope; they knew how much their parents loved them and how hard they were trying to get home. But not everyone feels so hopeful during the holidays.

Give someone else hope. Remember the song "I'll Be Home for Christmas" and think about the deep yearning in the words, how much the singer longs to be home if only in his dreams. Just like the many soldiers who've sung this song during times of war, there are many at Christmastime and in other months of the year whose lives are empty and lonely. Loneliness is what causes more people to lose hope than almost anything else. It's not a lack of money or the loss of a job that causes someone to feel hopeless, it's the lack of people who care.

Think about someone you know who might be feeling lonely or hopeless and contact that person. Pick up the phone and call someone you haven't talked to in more than five years. You'll be surprised how grateful he or she will be and what it will do for your own spirits.

The Search for Mary

HELEN KINZELER

*"There has been only one Christmas—the rest
are anniversaries."*

—W. J. Cameron

Everything was ready for the most wonderful time of the year. After weeks of preparation, golden reindeer and a sleigh nestled on the mantel amid fresh-cut greens enhanced by dozens of glittering lights. Santas graced the piano, while garlands and ribbons adorned the stairway.

The Christmas tree was lovely, laden with precious ornaments collected over many years, and tiny red lights twinkled among the soft branches. Under the fragrant tree, piles of gaily wrapped gifts awaited the eager fingers of children. The house was filled with the delicious aroma of homemade cookies and candies and the heady scent of pine and fir.

But one thing was missing. The mystery, the miracle, and the wonder of the spirit of Christmas had not entered into my heart. A wise person once said that miracles are for believers and that miracles are the soul of Christmas, which is love. If we have the spirit, we know it, but when it eludes us, we hunger and long for it.

My one hope lay in the ceramic Nativity set I had been working on for months. It was in its final firing and would be ready by six o'clock in the evening of the day before Christmas Eve, and I could not be late. That day had now arrived. I thought that maybe when the beautiful, creamy-white pieces were in place in our bay window, the Christmas spirit also would arrive.

A blinding snow and ice storm raged outside with a biting, slashing wind, and darkness was settling in earlier than usual. It was already past five o'clock, and my eighteen-year-old son and I were just leaving to brave the slippery drive to the ceramics shop when the phone rang. The voice on the other end of the line sounded feeble and desperate.

"This is Alice, your neighbor," the quavering voice whispered. "I dropped a glass of water in the kitchen, and the glass broke, and I cannot see to clean it up. Please help me."

Alice was the elderly lady living next door. Almost blind and deaf, she had been unable to get around without a walker since fracturing her hip. At that moment I did not want to help her, but because she used that most powerful word, "neighbor," I had no choice.

The mess in her kitchen was worse than I expected. The glass had shattered, and shards and splinters were everywhere. While I crawled on my hands and knees mopping up the water and picking up pieces of glass, I could feel Alice squinting at me through her thick lenses as she stood nearby clutching her walker with severely crippled arthritic hands that had once glided effortlessly, magically, over piano and organ keys, bringing untold delight and joy to many. Her feet and ankles were swollen and misshapen now, yet once she had danced. She was well over ninety years old, childless and widowed, but still proud and intelligent. It must have hurt her to call for help.

When I left her, only ten minutes remained before the deadline at the ceramics shop. Luckily, there were only a few other drivers braving the storm. One block from our destination, we saw a station wagon stalled by the side of the road, distress lights flashing, and a girl standing in the snow, frantically waving for help as we inched past her.

Then my son shouted, "I know that girl! We must help her!" Before I could protest, he was out of our car and at her side, returning in a few minutes to explain that the car was out of gas, that he would drop me off at the ceramics shop and return for me as soon as he helped his friend get on her way again.

It was after six when I reached the shop, and the shade was drawn on the entry door with a CLOSED sign attached. I pounded on the glass with frozen fingers.

A faint light was visible around the edges of the shade, and finally the owner peeked out. Her face was angry as she reminded me in a cold voice that I was late. Then she closed the door as I waited in the snow and wind for her to slide two large boxes down the steps into the parking lot.

When we reached home we started unpacking the pieces carefully. They were so lovely, so smooth, so creamy white. Gently we placed them in the bay window in the dining room. First the shepherds and sheep, followed by the oxen and the donkey, the wise men and camels, and the angel that would hover over all.

Last, we set out the Holy Family. There was Joseph and then the Child and his little manger. But where was Mary? In disbelief we checked each piece again, shaking out the shredded packing material, scattering it on the carpet. The second-most-important piece was not there.

With a sinking heart, I called the ceramics shop and listened to the phone ring and ring. She had to be there! Finally she answered in a weary voice.

"Mary is not here," I said.

"She has to be," the exhausted voice replied. "Look again."

"I did, I did," I insisted. "She is not there."

"Wait," she said. After what seemed like a long time, I heard her say with great sadness and dismay: "Missed her somehow when I fired the others. I will have her ready the day after Christmas. Come back then." She hung up the phone, and even though I dialed over and over, there was nothing but the ringing.

The next day was Christmas Eve. The snow was still coming down, so I left home a little earlier for my job as a nurse at the long-term-care facility a mile away. I knew some of our staff members would call to say they couldn't come to work because of the bad weather and the holiday bus schedule, and others just would not come.

As expected, there were fewer workers than usual to care for more than one hundred patients. All of us worked as a team, feeding, turning, lifting, and bathing. We helped cook, wash and fold laundry, mop floors—anything that needed doing.

All the women were dressed in their prettiest clothes, their hair combed and curled, makeup applied to wrinkled faces. All the men were nicely dressed and cleanly shaven. We sang Christmas songs to them, songs from their childhood. Some joined in ever so sweetly. Most of all, we comforted them. We talked to and touched each person. We listened to their Christmas memories, to their losses. When the shift ended, we clocked out, but some of us stayed to make sure everyone would be served a nourishing meal and be put to bed on clean sheets when it was time.

By the time I left to go home, the snow had stopped and the wind was gentle. The world seemed clean and soft in the pristine silence. It was transformed into a beautiful wonderland, its rough edges smooth, its scars and wounds hidden. It was very cold and clear, the kind of night that made countless stars visible. I wondered if the shepherds had seen these same stars that first Christmas.

I realized that night that the miracle of Christmas comes when least expected. The wonder, the awe, and the mystery come silently when there is room at the inn in our hearts, when our wants and deepest longings are put aside to embrace the needs and longings of others:

"This is Alice, your neighbor," the feeble voice had entreated.

"I know that girl! We must help!" said our caring child.

"I missed her somehow," the craft-shop owner had said sadly.

All these were viewed as obstacles, as stumbling blocks, when in reality they were guideposts leading me to Bethlehem, to the miracle of Christmas.

When I was a little girl, an old nun who taught us religion told us to keep our eyes on the star—not only at Christmas but all our lives—and we would never lose our way. In the hustle and bustle of preparing for Christmas, it is easy to lose our way, to lose sight of the star and miss the miracle.

Later that evening, while my family and I listened to carols, the peace and quiet were interrupted by the ringing of the doorbell. Not expecting anyone, we wondered who would be out in the cold on Christmas Eve.

I opened the door, and in the darkness I saw the owner of the ceramics shop, still wearing her paint-spattered apron. Her face was lined with exhaustion and a kind of radiance, and her eyes were filled with joy and light. We looked at each other, two believers who had found the miracle of Christmas.

In her hands partly concealed by an old rag, was Mary: perfect, beautiful, creamy white. In silence she handed Mary to me, our hands touching for a moment.

"Merry Christmas," she whispered as she vanished into the starry night.

✫

Searching for the magic of Christmas, one woman's hope was restored by the radiance of a simple, ceramic figurine. As you decorate your home and hang ornaments on the tree this year, reflect on the meaning of some of the traditional symbols of Christmas. Then make room in your heart to embrace the wonder and beauty of what they each represent.

> *Fir tree: The evergreen color represents the everlasting hope of mankind; the needles pointing upward symbolize man's thoughts turning toward heaven.*
>
> *Star: The heavenly sign of promises long ago, the shining hope of mankind.*
>
> *Wreath: The eternal nature of love, never ceasing, forming one continuous round and having no end.*
>
> *Candy cane: The shepherd's crook or staff, used to bring lost sheep back to the fold.*

Gifts: Symbolic of the gifts brought by the wise men to
  the Christ Child.
Bells: Ringing out to guide lost sheep back home, suggest-
  ing guidance and return.
Gift bow: Tied as we should all be tied together, in
  bonds of goodwill and brotherhood.

Although these are the symbols of Christmas, we can still
focus on their meaning throughout the year as we catch sight
of them. A flowered wreath on our neighbor's door in spring-
time can remind us of the eternal nature of love. The faint
sound of a bell or chime in the distance can call us back at
any time.

And then there is the star. The advice of a nun many
years ago is equally true today—all year long we should keep
our eyes on the star so as not to lose our way.

Let the Feasting Begin!

DR. DAVID GRAFTON

"So many gods, so many creeds; so many paths
that wind and wind,
While just the art of being kind is all the sad world needs."

—Ella Wheeler Wilcox

In Egypt, Christmas trees are almost nonexistent. They do show up in December, however, on street corners in areas where Westerners live. You can purchase a tall, spindly "Charlie Brown" Christmas tree for quite a sum, and many Western Christians subject themselves to the time-honored tradition of having such a Christmas tree. So, with mixed emotions, they shell out the large sums of money to erect a couple of pine branches stuck in buckets of sand in their homes to maintain some semblance of Christmas back home.

This last year our family shipped us a four-foot artificial tree. By some lucky stroke, our tree arrived in the mail after six months afloat on a boat in the middle of the Mediterranean. We actually were not expecting it and had written it off as "lost at sea," or at least lost to some fortunate customs official who liked the look of it. In any case, our tree arrived this fall and we were lucky to have a four-foot fake evergreen for Christmas rather than our usual tall, sparse, and spindly "Charlie Brown" tree.

We had just finished decorating our new tree with all the trimmings we had garnered over the past few years when the door bell rang. It was Ahmed, our taxi-driver friend, standing in his *gallabiyya* (a traditional long robe), which he wears during Ramadan, the Muslim holy month of fasting. Ahmed normally wears jeans and a sporty jacket when he drives his taxi around the city, but during Ramadan he dons a *gallabiyya* while he fasts. There he was, standing on our porch with a seven-foot, bushy green live Christmas tree.

Quite puzzled, I asked him about the tree. "It is yours," he said. "Happy Christmas. Can you come to Iftar tomorrow, Mr. David? Five o'clock?"

"Certainly," I said. Then he quickly waved a farewell and drove off. It was one of the fullest and greenest pine trees I had ever seen in Cairo! It certainly cost a good deal of money, especially for a man who undoubtedly makes less than seventeen dollars a day, which he must use to feed his family of six.

Ahmed is a Muslim from one of the poor areas of Cairo. Every evening he drives his taxi down the narrow, dirt-paved streets, ignoring pedestrians, cyclists with racks of bread on their heads, and children playing soccer with whatever they can dig up that will roll. He is what sociologists label as the backbone of the social stratum that supports the Islamic fundamentalists in Egypt: the poor, working-class Egyptians who have no future.

Yet, this man is no fundamentalist. He is no radical. He is a simple, loving man who shows his kindness by doing things like purchasing an expensive Christmas tree—an object that means little to him in his world—for a friend. He comes from a culture that the Western media portrays as rock-throwing, flag-burning, death-chanting, angry Arab Muslims. And I am what Islamicists call in negative terms a *mubashir*—a missionary. We come from very different worlds. We have very different world views. And the world has put a wall between us.

Ahmed invited us to an Iftar, a meal that marks the breaking of the Ramadan fast at sundown each day. Once we had zigzagged our way through the dusty, chaotic streets, we arrived at the building where he lived. He was on the first floor, his brother's family lived on the second. The goats and chickens lived on the roof. We were invited into his small three-bedroom apartment, where we sat on the floor of a bedroom. As sundown approached, plates of chicken and roast beef and trays of salads and bread were set before us. It looked delicious.

Within a matter of minutes, the small black-and-white television produced an image of the Citadel, the national fortress built by Saladin. Up on the ramparts of the Citadel, overlooking the city, a cannon fires every sundown during Ramadan, signaling the official end of the fast for the day. When the cannon roared over the television, Ahmed said, "Itfudal [Help yourself], Mr. David." And the feasting began.

It didn't take long until our three children had had enough chicken, rice, and bread. They quickly lost interest in adult conversation and became interested in Ahmed's children. Although they barely spoke each other's language, the children resorted to the language all children understand: playing games. Two of the three bedrooms immediately became playgrounds of activity, much to the delight of Ahmed's family. They started by devising a version of "Duck, Duck, Goose" and worked up to a rousing game of "Hide and Seek" in the small flat.

There we were, in the midst of a poor, Muslim section of Cairo, breaking the fast together, our children playing like the best of friends. There was nothing more human, more genuine, more poignant to the angelic host proclaiming "Glory to God in the highest, and on earth, peace . . ." than the laughter of children and the delight of adults in conversation around the table. It was an encounter that we usually paint in broad strokes: Arab and Westerner, Muslim and Christian, Islamic fundamentalist and Christian-imperialist missionary. But those broad strokes almost always miss the reality—and the beauty—of the true encounter.

Christmas is the most natural time to reach out to strangers, to the lonely, to the homeless, the widowed. Local colleges have lists of foreign students who are studying in the United States and will not be able to go home at Christmastime. These students would welcome a home-cooked meal over the holidays. Give your family an opportunity to be host so that Jesus' words "I was a stranger and you took me in . . ." can come true in your home this year.

Why not stretch the gift a little further into the year and benefit from the good feelings that come from being kind to strangers anytime? During other holidays—Valentine's Day, Thanksgiving, Easter—check with local hospitals, prisons, police stations, libraries, or nursing homes. They often appreciate homemade decorations or homemade cards to brighten their walls. Your acts of kindness will benefit those whose hearts are hungry for love and will warm your hearts as well.

The Rest of the Story

THERESA SCHAEFFER

"Such is hope, heaven's own gift to struggling mortals, pervading, like some subtle essence from the skies, all things both good and bad."

—Charles Dickens

I love Christmas stories. Every year I get out the same books for my children to read and browse through— *The Polar Express, The Night Before Christmas, The Gift of the Magi*—stories that, along with their magical illustrations, we all cherish and anticipate reading during the holidays.

But unlike these stories of Christmas fantasy and fiction, there is one story that my children especially love— because it really happened. It occurred almost seventy years ago, and although some of the characters in the story have since become famous, it's the story *behind* the story that my family loves most:

On a cold December night in the city of Chicago many years ago, a four-year-old girl named Barbara came to her father with an important question. It was asked out of a child's curiosity and not intended to hurt feelings, yet it deeply affected the child's father, Robert May. "Daddy, why is Mommy different from everybody else's mommy? Why can't she play with me like other mothers do?"

Bob May's eyes surveyed his shabby two-room apartment. On a thread-bare couch lay his young wife, Evelyn, weak and frail from cancer. For two years she had been bedridden, and for two years all Bob's emotions had been spent and his small savings had gone to pay for her treatments and medicines.

The terrible disease had already shattered two adult lives, and now it was having an effect on his growing daughter's happiness. As he smoothed his daughter's golden brown hair, he prayed for some reasonable way to answer her question.

Barbara's father knew only too well what it meant to be different. As a child he had been teased by playmates for being weak and sickly, and being called "skinny" and "shorty" often brought him to tears. Later in college, Bob May was so small that he was often mistaken for someone's little brother.

Bob's adult life wasn't much happier either. Unlike many of his classmates who went straight from college to impressive and high-paying jobs, Bob became a copywriter for the Chicago mail-order house, Montgomery Ward. Now, at age thirty-three, Bob was deep in debt, depressed about his wife's condition, and afraid to consider what lay ahead for his daughter.

Although he didn't know it at the time, the answer Bob May gave his little girl that night eventually made him famous and wealthy. It would also bring joy to millions of children just like his own Barbara. On that December night in the run-down Chicago apartment, Bob cradled his little girl in his arms and began to tell a story, making it up as he went along . . .

"Once upon a time there was a reindeer named Rudolph, but this reindeer was different from the others: Rudolph had a big red nose. Naturally, people called him Rudolph, the Red Nosed Reindeer."

As Bob went on to tell about Rudolph, he tried desperately to help Barbara understand that even though some of God's creatures are strange and unique, they often possess a special gift inside: the miraculous power of bringing joy to others. Bob hoped Barbara would see the comparison with the joy they had both received in the past from Evelyn.

Bob continued to explain that Rudolph was terribly embarrassed by his glowing, bulbous nose. Other reindeer laughed at him, and even his own parents were ashamed to take him out in public. So Rudolph moped around in self-pity.

"One Christmas Eve," Bob continued, "Santa Claus got all his reindeer—Dasher, Dancer, Prancer, and Vixen, Comet, Cupid, Donner, and Blitzen—ready for their annual trip around the world to deliver toys to all good little girls and boys. Everyone at the North Pole assembled to cheer these great heroes on their way. But this particular year a terrible fog covered the world, and Santa was afraid that the mist was so thick he wouldn't be able to find his way to anyone's chimney.

Suddenly Santa looked up and saw the answer to his dilemma standing right in front of him. Rudolph, his nose glowing brighter than ever that night, would provide just enough light to safely guide them! He quickly led Rudolph to the front of the team, fastened on the leather harness, and climbed in the sleigh.

They were off! Rudolph took Santa to every chimney that night with ease. Rain, snow, or fog—nothing held Rudolph back, for the glow from his bright nose penetrated the mist like a beacon.

And so it was that Rudolph became the most famous and beloved of all Santa's reindeer. The very thing that had made him different and caused such embarrassment was now the envy of every member of the reindeer community. Santa Claus shouted Rudolph's praises to the whole world, and from that Christmas until today, Rudolph has been living happily ever after."

Barbara giggled excitedly when her father finished. Every night she begged him to tell the story again, until finally Bob could almost recite it in his sleep. Then, at Christmastime, he decided to turn the story into a poem and put it in book format illustrated with pictures. He had no money with which to buy gifts, but Bob knew Barbara would love getting his story as her own personal book for Christmas. Night after night, long after Barbara had gone to bed, Bob worked on the verses, determined to finish his gift for his precious daughter.

Just as Bob was completing the project, his beloved wife died. Bob was despondent and turned to Barbara as his only source of comfort. Yet, despite his grief, he sat at his desk in the quiet, lonely apartment and completed his little booklet about "Rudolph" as tears clouded his eyes.

Christmas morning came, and Barbara cried with joy over his handmade gift. Even at her young age, she somehow knew that she and her daddy would survive as long as they had each other. A few days later, Bob was invited to an employee holiday party at Montgomery Ward's, and although he wasn't in a partying mood his office associates insisted. When Bob finally agreed to go, he took with him the poem and read it to the crowd. By the end of his reading, the crowd broke into thunderous applause. They had fallen in love with "Rudolph." That was in 1938.

By Christmas of 1947, six million copies of the booklet had been given away or sold, making *Rudolph* one of the most widely distributed books in the world. The demand for the book and for Rudolph-sponsored products increased so much that historians predicted that *Rudolph* would become one of the most famous stories ever to be told.

The historians were right. Bob May's Christmas tale would carry his daughter through sad and lonely times and bring joy and hope to millions of other children for many years to come.

✭

Bob May created a memorable Christmas story to remind us that, regardless of our individual differences, we all have something to contribute to a larger effort. It is easy to lose sight of our own talents and special gifts and to feel, at times, that no one appreciates us.

Sit down by yourself or with your family on a summer evening and watch the movie It's a Wonderful Life. *Try to watch the whole thing through—not the way you watch it in December when you catch glimpses of it between wrapping presents and decorating the tree. Listen to the wonderful dialogue and ponder its message. Why did George Bailey almost give up in despair, and what restored his hope? What does he count as his riches by the end of the movie?*

Think about your own life, or talk with your children about their lives and the people they've touched. Try to stand back, as George does in the movie, to consider the choices you've made, the people you've helped, and what the world would be like without you. Write down three people, groups, or situations you've positively influenced, and you'll begin to see more clearly your unique contribution to the world. It will help to convince you (and your family members) that you too have a wonderful life.

Radio Days

COOKIE CURCI-WRIGHT

*"My idea of Christmas is very simple: loving others.
Come to think of it, why do we have to wait for
Christmas to do that?"*

—Bob Hope

My childhood was filled with stories, stories that boasted colorful characters, lively dialogue, and wonderful settings. Best of all, each story taught a valuable lesson. Children's books, you say? No. Although I did my share of reading the beautifully illustrated fairy tales and nursery rhymes, the stories that filled my childhood were not written down. They were spoken.

Night after night as I lay in bed with the hand-stitched quilt drawn up under my chin, I listened in the dark as my mother, my father, a grandparent, a visiting uncle, or an older cousin filled the nighttime silence with stories of life in the Old Country, Italy, or even tell stories of life in the New Country—America.

I loved these family stories. Each one gave me a clearer picture of my ancestors, or a better understanding of relatives I already knew. One of my favorite nighttime stories was about my great-grandpa and his radio and how it helped him learn the real meaning of friendship.

Papa Vincenci nestled comfortably into his rocker and with a twist of his hand clicked on the dial of his brand-new RCA Victor radio. It was Papa's habit each night, after one of Mama Savadia's robust Italian meals, to position himself by his beloved radio and tune in to the nightly antics of radio characters: Fibber Magee and Molly, Amos 'n' Andy, Edgar Bergen and Charlie McCarthy, and the Lone Ranger.

There were no complexities in Papa Vincenci's lifestyle; his wants and needs were easily satisfied by a good meal, a warm home, and a loving family. He lived by the simple, old-fashioned creed "Pray for the things you want, work for the things you need."

If Papa had one luxury, it was the household radio he had acquired. The radio had become a vital component of his daily life. It restored his energy and brought back his sense of humor after a long day working as a tree pruner in the fruit orchards of the Santa Clara Valley. With the impending arrival of World War II, the economy had begun to tighten, but the budget-wise grandfather had managed to scrimp and save enough money from his meager earnings to purchase the new radio. Although Papa had known poverty in the Old Country, he'd never felt poor, only broke. Being poor, Papa believed, was a state of mind; being broke was only a temporary situation.

Papa loved his new radio, but Great-Grandma preferred listening to her old Victrola or puttering around her woodstove to sitting by the radio—until the day she heard her first episode of *One Man's Family* on NBC radio. This show was about a strong, loving family, something Great-Grandma could relate to. From that moment on, she was an ardent fan of the new medium.

In time, Great-Grandma came to believe that the radio had been sent to them as a blessing. It had helped both her and Papa Vincenci to learn better English, and it had been a boost to their social life as well. The radio gave them something in common with their neighbors, who listened nightly to the same programs.

On warm summer nights, Papa sat on his front stoop with his neighborhood cronies, Mr. Goldstein, Mr. Miller, and Mr. Rosenberg, discussing their favorite radio programs. There were times when Mr. Goldstein would explain the meaning of a certain Yiddish word Papa had heard on the Molly Goldberg show. Other times, Papa would translate a Puccini opera for Mr. Goldstein. Some nights the old friends had a good laugh at the expense of the contestants on Ted Mack's *Amateur Hour*. The radio helped to bond these old friends, who came from vastly different backgrounds, in a way few things could. These men had left their native lands to escape tyranny and oppression, and as young immigrants they settled into the neighborhood together. Although they came from varied parts of the world and had different religious beliefs, they shared a love for their new country and for family traditions.

And so their friendship grew, until that fateful December day in 1941 when Papa's radio brought him the terrible news that Pearl Harbor had been attacked. He heard President Roosevelt declare war with Japan and with the Axis powers, Germany and Italy. It was a declaration that would change Papa's life.

The knock on Papa's door came early on a December morning in 1941. It brought with it a special-delivery letter from the U.S. government declaring that Papa must surrender all radios on his premises, effective immediately! All people of Italian heritage who lived near the East Coast or West Coast were subject to this ruling. The American government was worried that shortwave radios would be made out of home radios and that vital secrets might be passed to the enemy.

Papa Vincenci had no political ties to his former country. He had worked and lived in America for more than thirty years and had raised his children and grandchildren as honest, hardworking U.S. citizens. But the fact remained that he was a native of Italy, a country now ruled by the fascist tyrant Benito Mussolini, who had chosen to side with the Axis powers against the United States.

As Papa read the dispatch, tears of indignation rolled down his face. Losing his radio would be sad enough, but Papa was more concerned that he might lose the company and the respect of his friends in the community, which he had earned over thirty years. More than anything else, Papa prided himself on his honesty and high moral standards. His word had always been his bond. Now a war thousands of miles away had cast a shadow over him.

It appeared that Papa's fears were well-founded. Some of his employers, leery of Italian immigrants, had begun canceling their job offers. Papa worried that his longtime friendship with the Goldsteins, the Rosenbergs, and the Millers was also in jeopardy. Would they also view him differently now? Could they somehow believe that he shared the same political beliefs as the terrible tyrant Mussolini?

That Christmas Eve, Papa and Great-Grandma sat quietly in their favorite chairs, warming themselves by the fire. Papa couldn't help but miss the raucous sound of his radio, and the daily banter with his friends and neighbors, which he feared he had now lost as well.

A knock on the door brought Papa to his feet. Opening the door, Papa was surprised to find his old pals the Goldsteins, the Rosenbergs, and the Millers standing on his front stoop.

Mr. Goldstein was the first to speak up. "Vincenci, my friend. The United States government says that you can no longer own a radio. Is this correct?"

With a quizzical expression, Papa answered, "Yes . . . yes. This is so."

"But the government did not forbid you should listen to a radio, correct?" inquired Mr. Rosenberg.

"Correct," Papa answered.

Papa's neighbors handed him a sheet of paper. On the paper was a handwritten schedule listing the broadcast times of all his favorite radio programs. Each entry corresponded to a neighbor's address. His old pals had gotten together and worked out a radio listening schedule for Papa and Great-Grandma that included every show from *The Goldbergs* to *Little Orphan Annie.*

"Read it, my friend. It's all there," said Mr. Rosenberg. "You and the missus will listen to *Fibber McGee and Molly* at the Millers' house. Tuesday: Ted Mack's *Amateur Hour* and *The Goldbergs* at my house. Wednesday: *Edgar Bergen and Charlie McCarthy* at the Goldsteins'. Thursday: *The Lone Ranger* and *Jack Armstrong* at the Smiths' house, and so on, until all your favorite programs are accounted for. You won't miss one of your favorite shows if we can help it, Vincenci."

Papa's eyes welled with tears, but this time they were tears of joy and gratitude. Papa invited his dear friends into his house to celebrate. While Great-Grandma served freshly baked biscotti, Papa filled each glass with home-made red wine.

Before going to sleep that night, Papa and Great-Grandma said a silent prayer of thanks. Papa had lost his valuable radio on that somber day in 1941, but what he'd found in friendship that Christmas Eve was truly priceless.

✭

The friendships we develop in our own neighborhood can add richness to our daily lives and give us an opportunity to reach out to others nearby. The opportunity to extend a hand of friendship is needed now more than ever before. We live in turbulent times, where political and world events have an impact on each of us in a way we never thought possible.

Is there someone in your neighborhood who feels ostracized because of their family heritage or religion? In "Radio Days," the neighbors banded together to make someone feel included even after the political tenor of the times set them apart. Why not host a block party and encourage everyone to bring their traditional family dishes from generations past? Think of the amazing culinary array that will result!

Recycled Gifts

ALISA DANIEL

> *"To love means loving the unlovable. To forgive means pardoning the unpardonable. Faith means believing the unbelievable. Hope means hoping when everything seems hopeless."*
>
> —Gilbert K. Chesterton

I was sorting through some boxes when I came across an old, disheveled one labeled "M. H. Third Grade." My daughter came into the room and knelt down beside me.

"What's in the box, Mom?" she asked as she lifted the tattered lid. Inside was a small, broken child's teacup and saucer, an ink pen, a dirty white hair bow, a pair of soiled arm sweatbands, and an apple-shaped pencil holder with "#1 Teacher" on the front.

"Why are you keeping all this nasty, broken stuff?" my daughter asked. "It looks like a pile of trash."

"Oh, this isn't trash, honey. These are treasures from the hearts of some of my most precious students," I replied as I let myself slip back in time.

We had just moved to a new town because of my husband's job. I was the new teacher on the block, and a common policy was to give the new teacher a class she'll never forget—if she lives through it.

I was given a remedial third-grade class, which was fine with me. I'd taught second grade for four years, so I didn't expect it to be too much of an adjustment. I began to have serious doubts during my preplanning, however, when the teachers from down the hall would stop by my room, shut the door, and tell me how sorry they were that I was getting so-and-so from their class. Some even left in tears, letting me know that, for the record, they had nothing to do with setting up my class. Young and naive, I thought I could handle anything. How bad could it be? The kids would be eating out of my hand in no time at all.

On the first day of school, in walked the biggest third-graders I'd ever seen. Donte, weighing in at 225 pounds, could easily have made the first string on a high school football team. He looked me straight in the eye with a glare that said, "I hate school and you can't make me learn." Sedrick, tall and lanky with an attitude in tow, looked down at me. His favorite words turned out to be "I can't do that," delivered in a long, drawn-out whine. I began to get nervous as more children sauntered into the classroom. With the exception of two bright-eyed and innocent-looking girls, all the kids seemed troubled, old for their grade, and full of anger.

Latikka, the thief, stole from everyone, including me. David, the fighter, brought in a knife to kill Sedrick because Sedrick had said something about his mama. Lindsay, the quiet one, cowered in the corner, hardly ever saying a word—which was probably not a bad idea, considering the possible risks.

My delusions of grandeur dissolved instantly. From that day forward, I left school crying and exhausted from the stress of just trying to keep the kids from killing me or one another.

As time went on, I discovered that every child, except for two, had been retained at least one grade-level. In fact, most had been retained every year since kindergarten. The majority were twelve or thirteen years old and still in the third grade.

Determined, I went all the way back and pulled from my kindergarten and first-grade teaching tactics. I read from every good literature book that I could find on their grade level. I used learning centers for social skills and had them write in journals. I realized that these kids needed much more than academic skills—they needed love, compassion, patience, and a sense of hope for the future.

We worked on attitude and self-esteem. Every morning I told them that they were intelligent and wonderful kids and that I was proud to have them in my class. I focused only on their strengths, ignoring everything but weapons and physical assaults. We role-played ways to work through conflicts, and I had them write about their feelings. Over time, we read dozens of books and wrote pages and pages in journals.

By December, I was beginning to see an improvement in the kids' attitudes and behavior. For every day that we made it without major disruptions, I rewarded them with little prizes. If we made it for a week, I had a class cooking activity—and those kids loved to eat!

But as the week before Christmas break arrived, there was a noticeable change in some of the students. They seemed more negative and quick-tempered. We talked about the coming holidays, and they appeared extremely interested in what I would be doing. I told them about my children and how we would be going home to my parents' house and opening gifts with the family. The more I talked, the quieter the class became.

Suddenly, I realized what a fool I'd been. Many of these kids didn't share similar holiday experiences. Their homes were often not warm and caring, gifts were not abundant, food was not plentiful. Finally, Lindsay, the quiet one, asked if I was going to give them a gift.

"Yes, of course," I replied.

Sam asked what I wanted for Christmas. Latikka asked if I was going to be mad at her because she couldn't buy me anything. Others joined in with similar concerns. It became apparent that they were worrying about me—they were upset because they couldn't afford to buy me a gift.

"Well, I love cards and letters more than anything," I reassured the class. I set aside time for them to create special cards for me to be opened at our party on Friday, and the mood of the class picked up considerably. Small groups gathered in whispers, and soon everyone had projects going.

On the day of our party, everyone came together for the gift-opening activities. I gave each of them a book, a new journal, and a pencil decorated with holiday images. The children gathered around as I began to read the cards they had made. It was hard to choke back the tears as I read each special message—every one deeply meaningful and from the heart.

As Lindsay handed me her card, she also gave me a small object wrapped in toilet paper and paper towels. Inside was a broken child's teacup and saucer. She said it was her favorite and that she had found it when she was little. She wanted me to have it for my morning coffee. Sandy handed me a gift wrapped in paper recycled from the books I had given them earlier. Inside was a white bow for my hair. It was soiled from lots of wear, and the ends were frayed. I told her I would save it to wear for special occasions. Sam handed me an unwrapped red, apple-shaped pencil holder with "#1 Teacher" on the front. His mom had taken him to the flea market and he had spent his saved-up allowance on it. He beamed as he handed it to me.

Finally, Latikka handed me a gift wrapped in construction paper from the art table. As I unrolled the paper, an expensive blue Cross pen rolled out. It was the same pen she had stolen from me earlier in the year. She told me how she had bought it from a local store, and of course I said "Thank you." I was, after all, grateful to have it back.

As usual, I went home and cried. I had tried so hard to give these children a glimmer of hope during those months—hope for what they could become if they really wanted to. But in the end, they gave much more back to me. My tears that December day were because of the love these children had demonstrated in the best way they knew how—by giving me gifts from their heart, gifts that I will treasure forever.

★

A determined and devoted teacher gave the children in her classroom hope simply by believing in them. We all have the power to lift and inspire, to give hope to the hopeless, and usually it takes only a small word or gesture. Develop the habit of love and compassion by trying some of the following:

Think of reasons people do and say the things they do. Give them the benefit of the doubt when there's a misunderstanding.

Practice becoming an active listener. When talking to people, pay attention to their full message instead of just the words they speak.

Once a week, talk to someone whom you don't know. Decide ahead of time to look for their strengths and to reflect love back to them. Be happy for the success and accomplishments of others rather than feeling competitive or jealous.

Sit in a busy place once in a while and watch the people: their faces, their nonverbal language, their interactions with others. Try to imagine what their challenges and burdens might be.

Take on "the look of love." Try to look at others in a way that they know they are loved even if they have no idea who you are.

A Gentle Reminder

GARY KLEIN

*"Somehow Tim gets thoughtful sitting by himself so much,
and thinks the strangest things you ever heard. He told me,
coming home, that he hoped the people saw him in the
church, because he was a cripple, and it might be pleasant
for them to remember upon Christmas Day, who made lame
beggars walk, and blind men see."*

—Charles Dickens, *A Christmas Carol*

Loneliness coupled with Christmas can be an unbearable combination. Time seems to stand still, and getting through New Year's Day becomes the main objective. This is how I felt several years ago when my first girlfriend, River, broke up with me just before the Christmas season. I was devastated. Her timing was especially bad too, because my extended family was all gathering together in my hometown in Wisconsin, while I would remain alone in my California home.

Despite signs of holiday cheer all around me, my mind was flooded with self-doubt and a sense of rejection.

Being in a wheelchair increased my feelings of being unwanted and unlovable by anyone, especially someone of the opposite sex. Loneliness had completely overwhelmed me, and I desperately needed freedom from its clutches.

I cannot recount the number of times in my life that I've been told by a woman that I was the closest male friend she had ever had. But because of my handicap, all the women I had fallen for had eventually rejected me. This time it was different, and the months before the breakup were amazing. River was the first woman in my life who had made me feel lovable and attractive as a man. I felt accepted as I was, wheelchair and all. In fact, the times we spent together made my handicap a distant memory. For the first time in my life, I was loved—or so I thought.

After a few months, we came to a crossroad. While I wanted our relationship to grow in depth by getting to know each other's personality—to be able to express and understand more fully our thoughts, feelings, hopes, and dreams—River wanted a physically intimate commitment as well. Naturally, I desired this too, but I felt that we needed a stronger emotional foundation on which to build before taking that step.

Many people would consider my thinking old-fashioned, and as it turned out, my girlfriend was one of them. When I told her I wanted to wait until marriage before becoming more intimate, she left me within the week. The blow was crushing and crippling. In my despair, I realized my chances of finding someone else who could fully accept me and love me romantically were close to nil.

During the weeks after she left, I cried out to God frequently. I pleaded with Him to give me focus and direction. I begged Him to take away the pain and help me forget River. I just wanted to be numb.

A few weeks before Christmas, I found myself driving with no destination in mind. My feelings of rejection and loneliness had become a constant dark cloud over me, and I was frustrated with my lack of purpose and direction. That night was a bit different from the others, as I felt compelled to ask God to use me in someone else's life. Perhaps that would take my mind off my own grief. Shortly after the prayer, I found myself stopping at a local grocery store with nothing in mind to buy.

As I entered the store, I decided to roam the aisles to find something to purchase. After a few minutes, I was startled by a loud crash of breaking glass in the aisle next to mine. This was followed by several more crashes, and then two women began yelling expletives at each other. People's conversations immediately lowered to a quiet murmur, and I noticed everyone scurrying away from the general direction of the women.

My heart raced with anticipation and concern. Something inside was urging me to help them, and I started heading down my aisle, turning the corner toward theirs. The women were obviously enraged, and I had no idea if food would be thrown at me as well, but I was willing to take the risk.

When I got a few feet from these two young women, they both stopped arguing and looked directly at me. I knew I was going to talk to them. I'm not sure if it was their curiosity at my handicap or their shock that someone was confronting them, but their eyes seemed to invite me to speak. I had no idea what I would say, but a simple "How are you?" spilled out of my mouth. It was a rhetorical question, really, because I knew exactly how they were!

They contritely answered they were fine.

"You don't sound fine," I answered. "I heard you two fighting from the next aisle over, and I wondered what was wrong."

Stunned, they glanced at each other then back at me and replied that they were just arguing about a number of issues.

The next words out of my mouth were not my own but came straight from God. "Looking into your eyes, I can tell that you both love each other very much. Am I correct?" Even though I knew in my heart the words were true, I couldn't believe I was being prompted to say them.

Their response was even more shocking. They both began to cry. I felt compelled to inquire more about them and learned they were sisters in their early twenties.

Without prying into the cause of their conflict, I simply told them the following: "I want you to know that

God loves you so much and is grieved by your fighting. He cares so much for you and your relationship."

The two sisters began crying again, and I suggested they give each other a hug. Without hesitating, they embraced each other and then hugged me too. We talked for another minute, I wished them a Merry Christmas, and headed back to my van. I never purchased anything, but my shopping venture was complete.

Inside my car, I began to weep profusely. It was clear that God had used me in a way that I couldn't deny. As I sat pondering what had just taken place, I suddenly saw things with new perspective. I realized that if I had been in the same place at the same time but accompanied by my previous girlfriend, she would've objected to my interfering with the two women. The thought of this was crushing and at the same time incredibly liberating. If I were ever to make a lifelong commitment to a wife, she would have to not only accept me physically but also accept me for who I was inside.

My desire for a companion at my side has not diminished over the years. While it's been a great blessing to be a girl's best friend over and over, I still hunger for someone whose love transcends that level of friendship. What a joy it would be to have a wife who would allow—even encourage—me to go down some of the challenging and uncertain aisles in the marketplace of life, and still remain by my side!

Christmas was different from what I expected that year. Some of my loneliness dissipated as I gained new insight into the real meaning of the sacred season. I had always anticipated Christmas as a time to fill my own needs of friendship, companionship, and love, but a simple grocery-store encounter taught me that the best way to fill those needs was to be willing to be utilized by God in caring for others.

Since that night nine years ago, I have tried to make each Christmas season better than the last, seeking to be attuned to the needs of others. By doing so, my hopes will continue to be miraculously transformed into God's hopes for me.

★

Great satisfaction is derived from giving to others, even in the face of our own personal pain. Rising above our own wants and desires to bring joy to others develops our sense of brotherhood and compassion.

Decide ahead of time to give service in lieu of presents this Christmas. Giving "acts of kindness" instead of ties, jewelry, toys, and clothing one year won't be as devastating as it may seem, and it will most likely prove to be a memorable experience for your family.

Another way to emphasize service is to have family members pick names at the beginning of any month of the year and play "Secret Santa" for the whole month. Perform unexpected acts of kindness for one another—straighten someone's closet, do their chores, feed the pet when it's not your turn, make someone's bed, leave flowers or candy on their pillow, and so on, and then reveal who each person's "Secret Santa" is at the end of the month. Imagine how delightful this could be all year round!

An African Silent Night

PETER ADOTEY ADDO

"Have you seen God's Christmas tree in the sky
With its trillions of tapers blazing high?"

—Angela Morgan

Christmas must be coming," Grandmother exclaimed, "because the 'Fire on the Mountain' flower is blooming!" My grandmother was very sick, but there was more than a hint of excitement in her voice. Although the people in our village in Ghana had lost all track of time because of the war, we were feeling a bit hopeful as Grandmother spoke.

"It's a miracle!" she continued. "We must celebrate Christmas right away! The red-and-yellow flower of this tree blooms only at Christmas—it has been that way for generations." I was only eight years old at the time, but I was spellbound by her tale.

"Even the fire that engulfed our marketplace didn't destroy the tree. Let us celebrate the blessed birth of the baby Jesus!" she declared.

I can still see the beautiful, bright flower in my mind today, and I remember how its nectar had always attracted insects, making them drowsy enough to fall to the ground to become food for crows and lizards. Yes, even the soldiers who set fire to our village couldn't destroy our special "Christmas tree."

But how could this be Christmas—the time for celebrating the birth of the Prince of Peace—when we had known only war and suffering for so many months? Grandmother told us she was certain that this day must be Christmas Eve, but there was no sign of the usual holiday decorations, none of the happy anticipation that normally accompanied Christmas. Like everyone else, I felt only sadness at the devastation and destruction around me. I had been forced to grow up very quickly that year, and any hopes of a joyous Christmas were shattered many months before, when the "Army of Liberation" attacked our village and took away many of the young boys and girls.

As it turned out, Grandmother's instructions to celebrate the birth of our Savior were her last words. Showing us the beautiful flower of the Fire on the Mountain tree was her last gift, for she quietly passed away later that day. I wept over my grandmother and felt certain that Christmas would never come again in my entire life. How could I ever feel joy after such terrible losses?

I thought back to the Christmases of my early childhood and the wonderful memories surrounding them. How I longed to hear the happy greeting "Afishapa," meaning "Merry Christmas and Happy New Year," that was commonly heard in our village during the Christmas season. How I missed the beautiful Christmas music on the streets, the relatives and friends who would visit from all different tribes, the taste of traditional foods like rice, chicken, goat, lamb, and fruits eaten at our Christmas dinner, and the dancing and festive procession through the streets on Christmas Eve.

Christmas in our village had always been a time for gaiety and celebration, but also a time for religious devotion. We went to church, sang carols, and read the scriptures that reminded us of Jesus' blessed birth. But conjuring up these happy memories now only intensified the painful reality of our current situation. I had not yet been able to rid my mind of the horrifying images of that fateful night the previous April.

I could still see the many families in our village being torn apart by the angry soldiers that night, some even being killed right in front of us. Those of us who survived were forced to march for many miles without food, eventually becoming so hungry and weak that we lost all sense of time and place.

Miraculously, one rainy night we were able to escape, and after several weeks of wandering through the tropical forest we made our way back to our burned-out village. Starving and exhausted, we searched for other family members but found no one. I was glad to have my older sister to cling to, even though she remained in a state of shock and unable to speak since the night we escaped the soldiers' violence.

A month or so after we returned to our village, Grandmother explained to me that my sister was carrying a baby. I wasn't sure how that happened, but I suspected it had something to do with the abusive treatment of the soldiers. Maybe, I thought, that was why she was unable to utter any words— because of the horror of what she'd experienced.

No, this day didn't feel like any of my former Christmas Eves, and even at my age I knew that all the wishing in the world wouldn't change the feelings of despair and hopelessness in my heart. As I wallowed in my misery, mindlessly kicking dirt clods around with my bare feet, I was suddenly aware of several cars approaching our village, honking their horns as they got closer.

"Quick, everyone! Run to the forest and hide!" an elderly villager shouted. "It's the soldiers with their machine guns!"

But we quickly realized that the cars carried only ordinary travelers. Apparently, these people were on their way to their villages to celebrate Christmas with family and friends but had taken a detour when they heard rumors of land mines on the road, planted by the soldiers the past April. Their detour had brought them straight to our village, and when they saw our condition they were shocked and horrified. Many of the travelers began to cry as they saw the suffering and devastation all around us.

"Yes, it is true," one woman said, as she dried her tears and began sharing with us what little food they carried in their cars. "Tonight *is* Christmas Eve. And because circumstances have brought us to your village, we will stay and comfort you on this special night." Then, as we told them more about our struggle to survive over these many months, the travelers helped us build a fire in the center of the marketplace to keep us warm.

There was much I didn't understand because of my age, but one thing was certain: My sister's condition was worsening every hour, and although she still had not spoken a word, it was apparent that her baby would be born soon. I was so afraid for my sister because we had no medical supplies and no hospital, and it scared me to think what one more tragedy would do to my family at this time.

Finally, her pain became so intense that she could no longer stand up, so some of the travelers and the villagers graciously used some of their clothing to make a bed for her near the fire, and several women gathered around to offer assistance. I knew this wasn't how these good people had intended to spend Christmas Eve, but I felt certain they had been sent to us in our hour of need.

Before the night was over, my sister gave birth to a beautiful, healthy baby boy. I remember looking at his perfect, tiny body, with skin as dark as the night around us. As I looked up to heaven, the sky was ablaze with stars, and in my young mind I wondered if there was a special star shining down on this little baby tonight, like I knew there was for another baby boy long ago.

"Come, let us celebrate!" My thoughts were interrupted by a voice calling us together, as is the custom in Africa when a child is born. War or no war, we had witnessed a blessed event, and in the African tradition we sang and danced until the rooster crowed at six o'clock in the morning. Mostly, we sang Christmas songs, everyone singing in their own language. And for the first time, as we joined together in celebrating my nephew's birth, all the pain and agony of the past few months was forgotten.

With the light of dawn, one of the travelers gently asked my sister, "What are you going to name the baby?" Of course, the newcomer didn't realize my sister hadn't spoken one word since the horrible night our village was burned. But suddenly, overcome with the joy that only a new baby can generate, my sister spoke. Tenderly and lovingly she uttered, "His name is Gye Nyame," which means "Except God, I fear none."

Christmas morning had come to our village after all. Never before and never since have I felt more joy than on that day—even though there were no gifts, no bright, beautiful crepe paper decorations to adorn our houses, no chocolates brought by Father Christmas, no choir to sing the traditional carols. But in the midst of our suffering, we had finally been given the gift of hope.

My grandmother's life, which had ended the night before, was replaced by a new, vigorous life—a sign of hope for a brighter future. Like Grandmother's "Christmas tree" flower that had brought forth new life in spite of the devastation around it, a baby had been born on a cold night by the light of a starry sky and the warmth of a fire. Strangers had come bearing gifts—their food and the shirts off their backs—to provide warmth and comfort for the mother and swaddling clothes for the new baby. And my sister had been able to turn her pent-up fear into a mother's lullaby.

Yes, Christmas had come indeed. Hope had been restored to our little village.

★

There is no greater evidence of the majesty and power of God than the process of birth. Although tragedy and violence preceded the blessed event in this story, hope was restored to the people of the village, and their spirits were renewed by the miracle of birth.

Whenever possible, witness a birth of some sort, and expose your children to it as well. Visit a barnyard or a state fair to see the birth of a calf or piglet; watch the process of a puppy or kitten born at home, a bird hatching from an egg, or even a seed planted in a windowsill flower pot. Talk about the miracle of birth, emphasizing that the process requires time and patience for expansion and growth to take place. This can also lead to reflection on the birth of the Christ Child and the meaning of His subsequent growth and mission.

Spaghetti for Christmas

WALTER STEVENSON

"The star of Bethlehem was a star of hope that led the wise men to the fulfillment of their expectations, the success of their expedition. Nothing in this world is more fundamental for success in life than hope, and that star pointed to our only source for true hope."

—D. James Kennedy

I had never seen the spirit of Christmas so profoundly manifested in such unlikely circumstances as I did on Christmas Day 1943. I was in a British division that was part of the American Fifth Army in Italy. Casualties had been continuous and heavy since we had landed at Salerno. By December, we were advancing slowly north of Naples—cold, very wet, very muddy, quite weary, and a little homesick. Never had the prospect of Christmas seemed so bleak and far away.

In a lull in the fighting, we decided to take up position on a small farm. The countryside was deserted, so we were surprised as we opened the farmhouse door to find a farmer and his wife and seven children. They invited us to join them for evening soup.

God had protected them, the farmer told us. The younger children, ranging from two to fourteen, had been huddled in the cellar for days. Two girls had sores on their legs, another had been hit in the back by a piece of shrapnel, and the father's arm was injured. Most of the cattle had been killed, the barn had been burned, and the retreating soldiers had taken their horses, most of their food, and some of their household items. They had no soap, no medical supplies, and very little food, but the house was sound, they were together as a family, and they didn't want to move.

With their cooperation, we set up a command post in their house. I was a medical orderly, so our commanding officer told me to do what I could for the children. The entire battery was concerned for this family, whose Christmas prospects seemed bleak indeed.

Without telling them, we collected precious bars of bath soap, talcum powder, candy, and various odds and ends for the children and their parents. We found a small tree that had been uprooted; it was not a traditional Christmas tree, but we decorated it with silver paper and colored wrappers. When we had finished, it was the best Christmas tree we had ever seen, decorated with all the love those soldiers wanted to lavish on their own families. At bedtime on Christmas Eve, we could hear the children praying for the English soldiers and their families.

When we presented our gifts to the parents early Christmas morning, they wept with joy. That Christmas dinner was the first time any of us had had spaghetti for Christmas, and the first time any of the Italians had eaten English Christmas pudding. I will never forget the children's delight over such simple presents, and the hugs and kisses that brought tears to every eye.

The family couldn't speak English, and most of us spoke very little Italian, but we all understood the farmer's toast: "If the spirit that is here now could be in the hearts of all men, this war would never have happened."

For some of those soldiers, it was their last Christmas on earth, and for those of us who survived, it was certainly the most memorable.

★

The soldiers in this story transformed an uprooted and forlorn tree into a glorious Christmas tree. The little tree and the humble gifts around it were symbols of hope to this poor family, a confirmation that life would go on despite their hardships. Sometime during the year, plant a tree. If practical, plant a young evergreen somewhere in your yard so you can watch it grow and flourish through the years. It will become your family's personal living Christmas tree; nurturing and caring for it will help keep the spirit of Christmas alive throughout the year, and it will contribute to enriching the environment.

Another way to celebrate life and hope is to give a tree as a gift—for the birth of a baby, a wedding, a housewarming, a twenty-fifth wedding anniversary, a Christmas present, or even to honor and affirm the life of someone who has passed away, as a lasting tribute in celebration of their life. Gift trees can be purchased through www.arborday.org for as little as $3.00, but the gesture will be long-lasting and invaluable.

The Gift of Charity

They called him Captain Santa, and to the people of Chicago two hundred years ago, the white-bearded Captain Schuenemann was as much a hero as the man in the red suit.

Captain Herman Schuenemann was in the shipping business, but because of his special love for Christmas he came up with an idea to make Christmas a little brighter for the families in his favorite port. With five thousand evergreens filling his ship's belly, he made a yearly voyage from Michigan's Upper Peninsula to Chicago with a majestic cargo of Yuletide cheer. Every year, wide-eyed children holding the hands of parents and grandparents would flock to the dock of Captain Santa's "Christmas Tree Ship" to buy trees for fifty cents to one dollar—the cheapest prices in town.

Captain Schuenemann not only offered bargain prices but also generously gave free Christmas trees to churches, orphanages, and any family who otherwise wouldn't be able to afford one. Yes, his trees were a source of income for him, but the special magic of the Christmas Tree Ship came from the captain's charitable kindness in spreading holiday cheer to some of the city's neediest families.

On November 23, 1912, the captain's wife stood on the freezing Michigan shore waving good-bye to her husband, just as she had done for more than a dozen years. Although she knew he couldn't disappoint the thousands of people who anxiously awaited his arrival, she worried that this year the ship was sailing too late in the season.

Mrs. Schuenemann had no idea how quickly her husband and his crew would get caught in gale-force winds as the ship strained in Lake Michigan's turbulent waters. As the gale turned into a raging blizzard, the crew struggled to keep the schooner afloat, but the trees became coated with ice and snow bearing down with the full force of winter. Rescuers searching the following day found no sign of the boat or of any wreckage. The Christmas Tree Ship was gone.

Christmas in Chicago was a somber one that year. But it wasn't to stay that way for long. The following November, 1913, people stood in awe at Thompson's Landing as they watched another old, wooden ship being loaded with evergreens. This one, however, was chartered by a woman of remarkable courage—the captain's beloved wife, Barbara. With a blue spruce tied securely to the top of the highest sail—as had been her husband's tradition— she and her two daughters were bound for Chicago, where the city was waiting. You see, the people of the city had heard that Mrs. Santa was on her way.

For the next twenty-two years, Barbara Schuenemann and her daughters set sail in November to honor her husband's memory and his love of Christmas. And for all those years, they carried on the captain's legacy of charitable kindness by giving away free Christmas trees to the poor and needy and to churches along the shores of the big city.

With great pluck and spirit, these bold women affirmed what Francis Bacon had said three hundred years before: "In charity there is no excess." To the people of Chicago, the Christmas Tree Ship had become a symbol of hope and cheer; it would always be part of their holiday and part of their hearts. The Schuenemann women would help that spirit live on.

The Bible says, "And now abideth faith, hope, charity, these three; but the greatest of these is charity" (1 Corinthians 13:13). Why is charity the greatest of these virtues? Perhaps because, more than anything else, it extends our spirits—it increases our capacity to love deeply by relieving the pain and suffering and loneliness of those around us.

Charity is work of the heart. Though often quantified as an action, charity is actually a state of the heart that prompts us to care for and love one another. Most times, we are sharing intangibles that are not easily left on the doorstep but are easily deposited in the heart.

Christmastime provides ample opportunity for charitable acts, but our hope is that we may also more fully embrace this virtue in the summers and autumns of our lives.

More Important Than Santa

SUSAN S. SPACKMAN

"They err who think Santa Claus comes down through the chimney; he really enters through the heart."

—Mrs. Paul M. Ell

On the morning that Santa was coming to my daughter's school, Eliza woke up early and was ready hours before preschool started at eleven o'clock.

"Mommy, let's leave early today so we won't miss Santa!" she exclaimed, as she started putting things in her backpack. At about eight o'clock, Brenda, a young friend of mine from church, telephoned to see if I could take her to the doctor, because the person who was going to do it had the flu. Brenda, who was only twenty-four, had cancer. She was apologetic for asking, but she told me it was a routine visit and would only take twenty minutes. I was happy to help. Because the appointment was at 9:00 A.M., I was certain we'd be back in plenty of time for the Santa party. After all, Eliza was ready to go.

When I saw Brenda, she seemed to be worse than I remembered. She was so sick and frail that she couldn't walk without help; it took my breath away to help her into the car. When we arrived at the doctor's office, we found out he was going to be late.

By 10:00 A.M. I was starting to get worried—Santa would be at the preschool at 11:30 for just a thirty-minute visit. If I had known we'd have to wait so long, I could've arranged for someone else to take Eliza. I felt torn, knowing how much Brenda needed me yet not wanting Eliza to miss the biggest party of her school year.

But Eliza didn't complain. In fact, she sat by Brenda and talked to her about the pictures in the magazines. They had always gotten along well, and Brenda especially enjoyed spending time with Eliza because she was anxious to have a family of her own. At 10:50, Brenda finally went in to see the doctor. It seemed to take forever, and although I ached for Brenda, I was getting more and more concerned about the time. Finally, at about 11:15, I was rushing a weak and nauseated Brenda to the car. She could barely make it.

As I started the car, I said, "Just let me get Eliza to preschool, and then I'll take you home." I probably sounded slightly impatient.

Once on the freeway, I drove as fast as I could so Eliza wouldn't miss Santa altogether. Then suddenly, Brenda asked me to stop. I pulled over just in time for her to get out of the car, crouch down, and vomit. I got out of the car and stood beside her—she was so sick, and I felt helpless and frustrated. My daughter didn't say a word—she could see that we were stopped in freeway traffic with emergency lights flashing and cars zooming past.

Finally, Brenda was able to get back into the car, but by then it was 11:45 and I knew Eliza would miss the party. It seemed that I could do nothing for either Brenda or Eliza and I wanted to cry for them both.

Once at Brenda's apartment, we helped her get situated on the couch, where she could stay until her husband came home. I fixed her some broth, brought a bowl and some towels over to the couch, and then we left. In the car I had just started to apologize to Eliza when she stopped me and said, "Mommy, it's okay. Brenda is more important than Santa Claus."

I felt such love for Eliza as I heard those words. They put the whole morning into perspective and reminded me of what I already knew. Brenda *was* more important than Santa Claus, but it took the pure love of an unselfish child to teach me the lesson I would never forget.

★

Christmastime brings everything into focus—the love in the air feels almost tangible and helps us see more clearly, as

Eliza did, what's really important in life. That feeling hardly seems duplicable, but it is possible to create some of its magic throughout the year.

To feel just a little of the love of the season all year long, celebrate Christmas in small ways on the twenty-fifth of each month. Listen to Christmas music on February 25, burn cinnamon or cranberry-scented candles on April 25, bake wreath or star cookies for your neighbors on June 25, take the family photo for your upcoming Christmas card on August 25, read Christmas stories or start making homemade gifts on September 25. These little reminders will create warm feelings of love and generosity, establish a unique family tradition, and allow just a hint of the Christmas spirit to creep into your home throughout the year.

The Christmas Dad Would Have Wanted

CONNIE SHERWOOD

"We must not only give what we have, we must also give what we are."

—Désiré Joseph Mercier

It was almost Christmas—just one more day to go. The tree was up, lights were strung around the front window, and a couple of chickens had been purchased for Christmas dinner—not the usual fare, but it would do.

The traditional Christmas family gathering went as well as could be expected under the circumstances, and the church Christmas party had left the children happy. The gifts that would be exchanged this year were under the tree—all but one, that is.

That gift lay unwrapped in the top drawer of the dresser in Bonnie's bedroom. It was to have been such a fine surprise.

All summer the five children had secretly tucked away money they had earned. Bonnie had spent hours ironing; Stan, Dick, and Elwood had washed windows in the neighborhood; and even little Dennis had fed the neighbor's dog while its owners were on vacation. On Sundays the children had met in Bonnie's bedroom to count the pennies, nickels, and dimes that were slowly filling the jar, and Dick would tell them how much was still needed for the special gift.

Finally, the day had come to make the purchase: a wristwatch for Dad. No more would he need to finger in his vest for the old pocket watch. Now he could tell time like the other men in town, who only had to glance at their wrists. All the children had walked to the store that day to see the watch, beautiful and shiny in its new case.

The final touch was an inscription on the back. "Let's just put 'To Dad, from your children,' since that's all the money we have for the printing," said the oldest brother. And that satisfied all of them.

But that thrilling, exciting day when the Peterson children had bought the watch for Dad now stung their hearts with its memory. Dad had died of a sudden illness on November 2, leaving the family and community in a lingering state of shock. Despite her own grief, Mom had tried hard to keep the Christmas traditions and see that the things the children looked forward to were still done. The tree had been placed in its customary spot. The Christmas cookie baking had been finished the Saturday before. But the things Dad usually did were left undone: The cards from friends and relatives were not clipped to strings in the shape of a tree on the back of the living-room door, and no one had wound the string of lights on the porch railing.

The afternoon shadows were starting to appear that Christmas Eve when a light tap came at the front door. Stan opened the door. The boy who stood there must've been about his age. Stan had never seen the boy before. His clothes were unkempt, and his coat seemed too light for a chilly winter day. The boy held out a waxed-paper bag that contained a few pieces of homemade chocolate candy. "I'm selling candy. It's only twenty-five cents a bag. Will you buy some?"

Stan asked the boy to wait while he went to the kitchen and asked Mom if she would be interested in buying a bag of candy. Lyla Peterson peeked around the kitchen door and saw the little boy standing patiently in the doorway. She got her purse from the cupboard and looked first among her change; then, putting the quarter back, she took a dollar from her wallet and gave it to her son. "Tell him he can keep the change, Stan," she said.

The little boy's eyes lit up with surprise and delight at the sight of the dollar. He thanked Stan several times, turned, and headed down the street. Stan took the little bag of candy to the kitchen. His mother watched the boy out the window, then turned to her son and said, "Stan, go out and call that boy back. I want to talk to him."

Stan found the boy a few doors down the block. As he approached, the little boy looked scared, and when Stan asked him to come back to the house, the boy seemed crestfallen. He undoubtedly thought they wanted their money back.

Lyla Peterson sat on the couch across from the boy and started to ask him questions. Where did he live? Well, right now he and his family were "kinda camping under the overpass just outside of town." Where did they come from? "Arkansas." His dad was to get a job at the airbase here, but when they arrived, Dad was sick, and the job was given to someone else. Did they have any place to go? No, not until his dad got a job and they could find something to rent. Where did he get the candy? His mother had made it over a campfire, and the children were trying to sell it to buy food.

Lyla was overcome with compassion. She began to form a plan. "Go get your mother," she said, "and bring her here."

Later that afternoon, the boy returned with his mother. Lyla greeted the two warmly and began to ask more about the family and their situation. There were five children, about the same ages as her own. The father was still too sick to find work. The children weren't going to school. The family had been living on half-rotten potatoes they'd found in the rubbish behind a market.

"Come stay with us," Lyla pleaded, "at least over Christmas." The mother sadly but firmly refused the offer.

After much coaxing, however, she consented at least to come the next day for Christmas dinner.

After the mother and little boy left, the Petersons went into action. First, Elwood was sent to the store for two more chickens and a few more carrots; Bonnie scurried to the kitchen to start another Christmas pudding; Dennis was assigned the job of stringing the Christmas cards in the shape of a tree on the back of the living-room door; and Stan was set to work winding the lights around the railing of the porch. Lyla hurried out to the local five-and-dime store. Soon she was back with a bag under her arm.

That evening everyone gathered in the living room, and one by one many of the presents under the tree were given new tags—names of the children who were to be their Christmas guests. The few gifts Mom had purchased that afternoon were wrapped and tagged and placed under the tree. Far into the night the family bustled about, trying to get everything completed by the following morning.

It was hard to sleep that night at the Peterson home. Had any Christmas before been as exciting as this one? Was any family in all of Sacramento feeling the spirit of Christmas as they were? "I think this must be the kind of Christmas Dad would want us to have. I'll bet he is happy too," thought Stan.

The next day proved to be everything they had hoped it would be. Stan's heart filled with pride when he saw his mother, who thought no one else was watching, give the mother of the family one hundred dollars. (It was at least

20 percent of Dad's insurance money.) Yes, this was probably their most exciting Christmas.

"What," Stan wondered as he matured and started his own family, "could they do to bring this special spirit into their lives every Christmas?" The answer was easy. That's why Stan Peterson and his wife and children provide Christmas for a needy family each year. They don't usually find one like the family who was "kinda camping under the overpass just outside of town," but they find one. And when Stan thinks of how that family was able to find an old house to rent with the money Mom had given them, and how the father found employment (and eventually was able to buy a small farm near Sacramento), he feels the special Christmas spirit that comes with caring and loving and sharing.

Sometimes, too, he remembers that one special gift, unwrapped, lying in his sister's top drawer. In Stan's memory, it lies there still, untouched, a symbol of the greater gift this Christmas had given all of them.

★

It is all too easy to focus on the sadness and disappointments in our own lives, and to overlook those whose lives are even more challenging or desperate.

Instead of rushing to the mall the day after Thanksgiving, take your family to the local Salvation Army or a soup kitchen and help serve Thanksgiving dinners to the homeless.

In some cities, you'll need to sign up months in advance for this, so consider making arrangements the first part of September, but you can usually find an organization looking for volunteers this time of year (check age requirements too).

Thanksgiving is a natural time to reflect on your blessings, and it's a good experience for your children to see people in need, to more fully appreciate their own blessings. You'll come away much more fulfilled than if you had fought the crowds on the busiest shopping day of the year, and your children won't forget the experience.

Don't forget that shelters, food lockers, and soup kitchens need your help throughout the rest of the year too. Volunteering to help out anytime is also a wonderful way to spend time with your family helping others in need.

The Orange and the Tramp

Kathryn P. Fong

"As the purse is emptied, the heart is filled."

—Victor Hugo

I had never truly experienced the joy of giving. Oh, there were the usual gifts on holidays and special occasions, all of which were purchased with the usual care. But when did I truly feel the "spirit" that should accompany the expression? Where was the happiness that should reward the heart of the giver?

So far in my young life, it seemed, I had failed to give of myself beyond the call of duty, even though I prided myself in giving some degree of compassionate service: babysitting, chauffeuring, helping in a crisis situation. But these were mediocre extensions of myself that deserved only modest praise and approval.

Not that I was looking for a ripe occasion to be benevolent. Not by a long shot! Age twenty-two was a reasonably sound, selfish age. But time and fate were conspiring to give me an opportunity to change my attitude.

Christmas had come and gone—an ordinary holiday with much too much rushing about. Each day I rode the regular commuter coach from Hayward to San Francisco and joined the throngs of office workers hurrying to their daily routine of earning a living. I had trained my channels of sensory perception to shut down completely during my mechanized march to the office each morning. I neither saw, heard, felt, nor tasted anything. My hide was toughened to endure the pushing, jostling sea of people. I was a true San Francisco commuter; I enjoyed the unheralded distinction of being alone in the crowd. Certainly no one would dare require anything of me during this time of day.

Until I met him. "He" was not a real human being to me—but a decrepit, whiskey-guzzling wretch, a beggar with a stench that merited neither attention nor pity. He was dressed in typical panhandler ensemble: black trousers torn at each knee and with frayed cuffs; gray-green T-shirt complete with air-conditioning vent holes; a woolen shirt of undetermined color whose buttons obviously had come from someone else's shirt; and a thin, dirty jacket. A pair of wooden crutches supported his frail body. A worn baseball cap managed to keep some of the rain off his whiskered face.

My automatic pilot commanded me to jam my hands into my pockets, offering no small change for his extended hand. I also pulled down my rain hat to avoid seeing his pleading eyes and turned up my collar to muffle any of his requests for help. I held firm to the code of honor among the bands of commuters. I did not give in.

I quickly forgot this daily small interruption, only to have it repeated several mornings later. Then, one chilly morning as I passed the freezing beggar, my conscience began to stir and the Ghost of Christmas Past began to speak from the distance. I shifted uncomfortably and reasoned that I was not responsible for his human annihilation, that it was his error in life, not mine. Besides, what could I possibly do for him? I had no power to make him well and whole again. Yet the man's image pricked my cold armor sufficiently to form a chink right where my heart was. I had to admit I was sorry for the poor wreck.

And with this remarkable show of feeling, I expected my conscience to accept and withdraw. It didn't. When I walked into church on Sunday, I was smothered in feelings of hypocrisy and guilt for my lack of concern. Every conceivable emotion and virtue bullied me with salvos of Christian demands. Finally I responded to the promptings of my heart. I would help this poor creature.

But how? I could not help salvage his life by shoving money into his grimy palm. He would only ravage himself with more liquor. Well, then, how about food? That was it. I would pack him a hearty lunch. When was the last time he'd enjoyed a brown-bag lunch? The only thing he would carry around in a brown paper bag was a bottle. I wondered if he remembered what a ham and cheese on rye was like.

Carefully I coordinated my image of a big, hungry man with a solid meal, which I shoved into the refrigerator with satisfaction that night. In my prayers, I told my Father in heaven my strategy, as if He and I were plotting a surprise party.

Monday morning, as I approached the corner the old man had inhabited for nearly two weeks and prepared to extend my offering, my heart was pounding with the goodly rhythm of human kindness. And I was greeted by a blank wall. He had gone—walked out on me—deserted! This skid-row personality who had haunted me for nearly two weeks had dared to vanish.

In disappointment I quickened my step and began what I knew would be a rotten day. It was. And the next day too, and the next. Two weeks went by, and I had decided to forget about my act of charity. Then one day as I walked impassively toward the street corner, my eyes darted beyond the Don't Walk sign—and there he was! Nothing had changed. He was his old filthy self, staggering to support himself on crutches, his hand extended for the day's alms.

My first impulse was to ignore him. Besides, I had no hefty lunch to offer.

"But you have an orange in your purse," my conscience spoke.

"Yes, I do," I retorted, "but what would he do with an orange?"

"Give it to him and see," my conscience battled.

"No. No, I don't want to."

But my conscience took over and guided my hand to my purse to rummage for the orange. It was a great physical contest. I hesitated as I approached him, but in the end extended my hand and put the orange into his palm.

I paused and looked under the bill of the baseball hat. His eyes remained fixed on the orange for a second, and then slowly he raised his eyes to mine—the prettiest blue eyes I had ever seen, set in the filthiest face. They were Paul Newman–blue eyes, amid a network of livid red and white. His mouth began to move, but no sound came. I smiled. He nodded and clutched the prized orange to his chest. No words were exchanged. None were necessary.

There on the corner of Mission and Fremont Streets in the city of San Francisco, the spirit of giving, the Ghost of Christmas Past, and the angels who herald Christian acts applauded long and loud in my heart. The beggar had given me a great and treasured gift. I knew what it meant to give.

I took a long, deep breath and turned away, still smiling. My steps resounded on the pavement as I continued my trek. Suddenly my eyes were open to the street scene as I took in the sights and sounds of an early San Francisco morning.

★

Try fasting for one or two meals a month—or even one meal a week, if you're so inclined. When you voluntarily refrain from eating, simply by skipping breakfast and lunch occasionally, you will experience a small degree of the discomfort that those who go through the pain of hunger feel day after day. For a few hours a month, you will come to know the emptiness that accompanies want and need.

It is only when we follow the old Native American adage about "walking in another's moccasins for a day" that we can begin to understand how much hunger really hurts. This understanding will deepen our compassion and motivate us to help alleviate human pain and suffering wherever and whenever we can.

The Christmas Coat

George E. Raley Jr.

"Every charitable act is a stepping stone towards heaven."
—Henry Ward Beecher

Personally and professionally, the year 1991 was one of the worst of my life. I had sunk into a depression that only got worse as the end of the year approached.

The holidays were always a difficult time for me anyway; the demands of the season with its hustle and bustle never seemed to be worth the effort, and somehow Christmas never lived up to my expectations. I wanted only to hide out in my house. The necessity of shopping, visiting relatives, and attending holiday parties was torture for me and filled me with despair.

But the Saturday before Christmas was a beautiful day. The sun was shining and the sky was blue. The air was crisp and clean, and the temperature was in the fifties. It was more like fall—my favorite season—than winter, but it did little to lift my spirits. I decided to take a walk, hoping that the sun and fresh air would help dispel my gloominess.

I went to our hall closet to get my light fall jacket. As I searched among the jumble of coats and jackets, I noticed a winter coat that I'd picked up at a flea market several years earlier. The coat, while not expensive, was both practical and very large. I'm a big guy—six feet tall and two hundred and fifty pounds—and I could wear this coat over a sweater and sport coat and still have room left over. It was medium blue, all cotton, with a quilted lining. I had stuffed the coat into the closet after buying it and promptly forgot all about it.

But this day, as soon as I saw it, a small voice inside me said, "Wash it."

Strangely, I followed this thought and took the coat downstairs to our laundry room, where I ran it through the washing machine. Rather than use the dryer, I decided to take advantage of the nice weather and dry it outside on the line. Then I took my walk. Unfortunately, this did nothing to cheer me up.

Just before sundown I noticed the coat still hanging on the line and went outside to bring it in. The coat had cleaned up nicely and smelled wonderful after having been dried outside in the crisp December air. As I returned it to the closet, I wondered what had prompted me to clean it, but I soon forgot about it once again.

That evening a bitter-cold front moved in. The next morning I built a crackling fire in our fireplace, and my wife joined me to read the Sunday paper in our warm, cozy family room. In the local section of the paper I noticed a feature article about Sarah's House, a homeless shelter in our area. The article described the staff, the people who lived there, and the limited services the shelter was able to provide.

The story went on to explain that the shelter could accommodate only a limited number of men because of a shortage of beds and that the maximum stay for a man was thirty days. One of their current challenges was a man who would be forced to leave because of the thirty-day rule and turned out onto the streets in the cold of winter without a winter coat.

In spite of my melancholy state, I felt immediate empathy for the man, and a fair amount of guilt as I sat in my easy chair before a warm fire on this bitter-cold Sunday. My eyes grew wider as I continued to read the shelter's plea to anyone who might have an extra-large coat to donate before this man's departure. Feelings inside me began to stir as I thought of the coat that I'd washed the day before. I pondered the "coincidence." Suddenly the same undeniable voice inside said, "Call."

I dialed the number of the shelter and spoke to a pleasant woman who explained that, unfortunately, the article had not clearly stated their need.

"The article has brought in a slew of coat donations," the woman said, "but this man is huge, and a standard extra-large coat just won't be sufficient."

"I think I just might have what you're looking for," I assured her. Leaving my comfortable post by the fire, I got dressed, grabbed the coat, and told my bewildered wife that I was headed for the shelter.

I found the building with no difficulty, parked, and walked into the reception area. I waited while the staff dealt with a minor crisis—a can of paint inadvertently spilled by some active children. A woman finally asked if she could help me.

"I called a few minutes ago about the coat," I explained, and without saying another word I held up the padded blue jacket by the shoulders to show off its enormous size. The women in the reception area started cheering.

"Oh, how wonderful! At last! It's big enough, it'll fit!" I handed the coat over amid exchanges of "Merry Christmas! Thank you kindly!" I'll always remember the look of joy on their faces over this simple gift.

I have given and received thousands of gifts in my lifetime, but giving my coat that year brought warmth to my soul I hadn't felt in a long time. In that brief moment, I was outside my own personal misery, thinking only of someone else. Perhaps it was the anonymity of the gift, or maybe it was that I expected nothing in return, but that simple act allowed me to feel good about myself because I'd helped another.

I didn't know it then, but this simple incident represented a turning point for me in understanding my purpose in life. I pondered the "voice" that had led me to this place. Where had it come from? What was this all about? At the time, I had no relationship with God; I believed I was responsible for my own destiny and believed that I alone controlled the events of my life.

Unfortunately, the next year things got worse for me, and I became more isolated and desperate. At my lowest moment, however, that same "voice" returned and gave me the gift of guidance. Now I really began to listen to its counsel. No matter how bad things got, this guidance— which I finally accepted as coming from God—was always there for me. Over time, I developed a relationship with God around which I rebuilt all the other relationships in my life. The joy that came from giving of myself became the key to my inner peace and happiness. As I reduced or eliminated my expectations of others and focused on helping them, I was transformed.

Christmas too has been transformed for me. It has become a time for sharing God's love with those around me. Gone is the fear, the anxiety, and the apprehension that used to cause me such despair. The day I gave the coat away I knew that to the extent we give to others, the world responds in kind.

I never met the man who needed the coat. I hope that someday, somehow, he will know of the miraculous gift he gave me.

★

When it comes to acts of charity, it's unclear who gains more: the giver or the receiver. Establish the habit of charity in your home by creating a family piggy-bank. It can serve as a family "charity box" and should be kept visible all year long. Encourage family members to drop extra pennies, dimes, and nickels into a designated can or jar whenever they feel like cleaning out pockets, purses, or drawers or whenever they feel the desire to give to a worthy cause.

Every time the jar fills up, decide together how to spend the money on a charity (or rotate the responsibility of choosing how to spend it). It can be something as simple as buying warm socks and gloves for a mother and her children in a woman's shelter, putting together a dozen or so school kits to donate to a children's receiving home (crayons, pencils, paper, erasers, coloring books, stickers, small toys in a zipper bag), sending "care packages" to military personnel overseas, or mowing the lawn for a neighbor who is in the hospital. Any experience in caring and sharing from our own hearts and pockets deepens our sense of compassion for those who are less fortunate.

Santa and the Orphan

ROGER DEAN KISER SR.

"In faith and hope the world will disagree,
But all mankind's concern is charity."

—Alexander the Great

I was very excited, smiling from ear to ear. It was several days before Christmas, and all the children from the Children's Home Society Orphanage had been loaded up in several large buses. We were going to the Mayflower Hotel in downtown Jacksonville, Florida, to attend a Christmas party for underprivileged kids.

We stood obediently behind our assigned seats at the long tables covered with white paper until the man on the stage said a prayer. He then told us we could sit down. Within minutes we were each served a meal fit for a king—large pieces of meat, lots of green vegetables, two big puffy rolls with real butter—all piled high on glass dinner plates, something we had rarely seen. I ate until I could eat no more, and I remember thinking how wonderful it would be to go to bed every night feeling so full, without the hunger pangs I normally experienced.

As we gobbled our food, some of the adults and older kids took their place up on the large platform to perform a little Christmas play. Then suddenly, the lights dimmed and everyone got very quiet. When the lights came back up, Santa Claus walked out onto the stage!

The kids went wild with excitement—everyone began clapping and yelling, filling the hall with a joyous din. I was as excited as the rest of them, but I knew better than to yell or jump up and down. You see, Mrs. Winters, the head matron, sat only three seats from me. She had made it clear that we were to conduct ourselves in a proper manner and that there was to be no yelling and screaming. So I sat there with my hands tucked underneath my legs, trying as hard as I could to contain my excitement.

The kids from each different orphanage were led onto the stage one at a time, and each child was handed a wrapped gift by Santa Claus himself. "Please let me get a *big* present," I kept saying to myself. As the line got shorter and shorter, my turn finally came. Santa looked right at me, smiled warmly, and then gave me a wink. He then reached over and handed me a large box that had two gold ribbons on it. As I leaned over to take the box from him, I tripped and fell to my knees. Without hesitating, Santa bent over and helped me to my feet.

"Move along, Kiser!" yelled Mrs. Winters.

As I tried to get my balance, I leaned up against Santa Claus's leg and looked directly into his eyes. His face, less than an inch from mine, radiated all the love and tenderness I imagined would come from the face of a father, if I had ever had one.

"Can I hug you, Santa?" I asked him timidly.

But before he could answer, Mrs. Winters had snatched me up by my shirt collar and was pulling me away from the line of children. Santa stood up, raised his hand in the air, and yelled out, "Please, Ma'am! These are little children!"

Mrs. Winters never looked back. Still tugging on my collar, she kept walking and pushing me straight ahead of her until we reached the stairs of the platform. When we got back to the tables, I sat down in my chair and started to cry. Through my sobs, I occasionally looked up at the stage to see if my gift was still sitting next to Santa.

The party finally ended, and all the kids were herded back to the big yellow buses. As we lined up waiting to board, I looked longingly at the variety of gifts clutched by each child.

"Ho, ho, ho!" I suddenly heard coming from behind me.

As I turned around, there stood Santa Claus holding the same big box he had picked out for me when I was with him. He set the gift down on the ground beside me and then knelt by my side. He wrapped his arms around me and embraced me with the warmest hug I had ever felt.

"Am *I* a children?" I whispered to him.

"Yes, you're a *good* children," he replied as he pulled back and looked directly into my eyes.

When I looked up at his face I saw something that I was quite sure no one else in the world had ever seen. I saw that Santa himself had been crying.

★

"Santa" showed great love and concern for a little boy he had never met before, and he went out of his way to brighten the little orphan's day. Is there some simple way you could help another in need at Christmas—or any other time of the year?

Give anonymously. Performing good deeds without receiving recognition is a valuable exercise in character-building. Anonymity engages the freedom to contribute without expectation on the part of both giver and receiver, and if you have children it teaches them charity in its purest form. This can be done in a variety of ways and at many different times during the year.

Leave plates of Valentine cookies on the neighbors' doorsteps, ring the bell, and run; leave May baskets made out of milk cartons or strawberry baskets and fill them with flowers; leave an envelope with a twenty-dollar bill (or more) under the doormat of someone who is struggling. Even paying the toll for the car behind you at the toll booth can be a rewarding and fun experience, especially if your children are with you. Each time you give anonymously, you'll go away empty-handed perhaps, but your heart will be overflowing with the spirit of giving.

A Slice of Pumpkin Pie

Jaye Lewis

"Selfishness makes Christmas a burden,
love makes it a delight."

—Author Unknown

I can still hear the sound of spoons scraping across the tin pie plates as we ate our portion of pork and beans. I was only three years old, and it was the first Christmas I would remember. As a transient family looking for a new home in Florida, our family was going to have a particularly lean Christmas that year. In our meager surroundings, we battled roaches, spiders, and ants of biblical proportions. And there were mice too!

These were no ordinary mice either. They were confrontational, intelligent critters. They scurried about, evading all the traps, and when my mother went screaming after them with a broom . . . well, it's a shame video cameras hadn't been invented yet! She would swing around wildly, making everyone run for cover. To our amazement, the mice would just stand there, challenging her accuracy. She never did hit the varmints, but she managed to deck just about everybody else in the room. Finally, the mice got bored, I think, and they all went south. All but one.

Christmas approached, and my mother began to work her magic. Out of nowhere appeared a tree, and then out of hiding came the ornaments. My mother was very secretive, and she stayed up long into the night, working by flashlight. All of us slept in one room, Mom and Dad on the sofa bed, me in between, and my brothers and sister on the floor.

Christmas Eve dawned bright and clear, and savory smells from the old stove filled the air. My mother's cheeks were flushed from all her cooking and other mysterious activities. Somehow, she managed to come up with presents for each of us, but even at my young age I noticed there was no gift for her.

"Why isn't Santa Claus bringing you presents, Mommy?" I asked, worried that her feelings would be hurt.

"Oh, I'm sure there will be something," she reassured me in soft tones. "Perhaps there will be a special surprise from the Christ Child," she said, revealing her European roots.

My mother pulled pie after pie out of the tiny oven: apple pie brimming with cinnamon; pumpkin pie with just a touch of spice; mincemeat pie and raisin cake. One by one, the smells made my mouth water.

Near midnight we went to church, but I was more
excited about the delicious meal that awaited us back
home. I could hardly keep my young mind on the sermon the minister was preaching about God's love on this
special night. By the time we left the church, it was
Christmas Day, and all of us were intent on the feast that
we'd been so patiently waiting for. We tiptoed into the
house, mindful of our sleeping neighbors, and tumbled in
around the kitchen table. We gathered together for a
prayer of thanks for our lovely meal, each one secretly
grateful that the pies had gone untouched by insects or
rodents.

"Wait!" my mother exclaimed, motioning toward the
door.

There in the doorway to the living room stood a tiny
mouse. It had huge ears and a little pink twitching nose.
My brother lunged, but my mother motioned for him to
be still. The mouse never moved.

Then, as if on cue, the mouse darted into the living
room, heading for the big dresser. Quickly it scurried, as
my mother marched toward it with ominous eyes. This
was one mouse that would be caught on Christmas Day!

Mom slowly opened the bottom drawer of the dresser,
then the next and the next. And there in one drawer,
curled up together in a tiny cozy bed made from scraps of
material and bits of wool, lay a bundle of naked, sleeping,
newborn mice.

"We can drown them!" someone cried.

"We can stomp them!" said another.

"We could keep them," I piped in.

About that time, the mother mouse crawled up on top of the dresser and looked down at her brood. It was a perfect time to destroy them! They were vermin. They carried disease. It was, after all, the logical thing to do.

"But it's not the Christmas thing to do," my mother said with a knowing smile.

A hush settled over the room. My mother gently closed the dresser drawer and the mouse ran behind it, slipping into her little nursery. With a mysterious smile, Mom disappeared into the kitchen and sliced a small piece of pumpkin pie. She returned to the dresser and placed the gift on the floor out of the way. A glance passed from Mom to Dad—the official decree to leave the mouse family alone.

"This is my Christmas present," she said, "sent by the Christ Child. He was born in a stable because there was no room for him in the inn. It's a sign." My mother continued becoming more and more convinced as she spoke: "Well, there's room for him in our hearts, and I think there's room for this homeless little family too!"

No one said a word. We returned to our feast, and I sat pondering in my childlike way, admiring this incredibly romantic woman who wouldn't allow a little mouse and her newborns to go hungry on Christmas Day.

✭

Without a gift for her under the tree on Christmas morning, the mother in this story found joy and meaning in the simplest of nature's gifts—and was thankful. Gratitude gives our days a keener edge, and our lives a more gracious touch—no wonder Cicero called it "the mother of all virtues." Without gratitude for what we have, we are less likely to care for those who have even less.

Gratitude is simply a state of mind—one that can be learned and one that can be taught to other family members as well. During the month of November, bring out a "Thanksgiving cloth"—a plain white or light-colored piece of material—and place it on your kitchen or dining-room table. Provide permanent markers and encourage family members to write on the cloth things they are thankful for, adding to it whenever something comes to mind.

The list can include things like friends, climbing a mountain, a kitten's fur, watermelon, an A in Algebra, kissing, the Disney Channel, the smell of a rose—the list is endless, but the exercise will make you more aware of life's rich blessings.

Christmas Conspiracy

DONAVENE AHIER JAYCOX

"Christmas is a necessity. There has to be at least one day of the year to remind us that we're here for something else besides ourselves."

—Eric Sevareid

As the oldest child in my family, I had the privilege of being a co-conspirator with my parents for eight years in a remarkable Christmas adventure.

During the first few weeks of November, my mother would say to me, "Donavene, it's time to go downtown. Do you think the winter coats will be in?" When I was very small, I didn't understand why Mother would ask *me* if the coats were in, for how was I to know such things? I went along for the fun of it, though, as Mother made our day together very special, including a stop for lunch at a wonderful restaurant where I could order anything I wanted from the menu. I looked forward to this annual outing with only my mother for company.

Now, those were the days before malls and large shopping complexes. We didn't own a car, so in order to get downtown we'd have to walk almost two miles, braving the snowy, blustery Toronto weather to catch two different trolleys and finally a bus that delivered us to Eaton's. Eaton's was a large department store in the center of town, a bustling place with shoppers rushing around carrying loads of parcels.

Mother always managed to find the very coat she wanted for my father. I always wondered why my father got a new coat every year when he had a perfectly good one in the coat closet at home. It wasn't until I was about seven years old that I began to figure the whole thing out.

Every year Mother searched through the enormous racks of coats, looking for the perfect one that would protect Father from the harsh winter. It had to be a heavy, full-length, fully lined wool coat, and of course it had to be at the right price, for Mother had just so much money to buy it.

A winter coat with those specifications wasn't inexpensive. My mother worked many long hours as a silk spotter for a dry-cleaning company. She often worked overtime to accumulate enough extra income to purchase a coat for my father and a few simple Christmas gifts for us children. In those days, there weren't any dry-cleaning machines; all the cleaning was done by hand. It was exhausting, but Mother made me promise not to tell

Father she often felt weak and worn out after working long hours at the company. Her gift to him was truly a gift of love.

We didn't open our presents first thing on Christmas morning, as most families do. As soon as we woke up, we rushed to see what was inside the stockings that hung on the mantel, oohing and aahing over each little item. After breakfast we attended church as a family, singing carols all the way home and savoring every moment together. Father then bundled himself up and left us for a few hours to volunteer at the local mission center, which was a homeless shelter and soup kitchen for the unfortunate. There were mostly men there, and almost all of them were suffering from some degree of alcoholism. My father himself was a recovering alcoholic and had helped establish the Alcoholics Anonymous program in Canada.

While Father was gone, Mother cooked our Christmas dinner. My job was to set the table with our nicest silver, china, and tablecloth. I loved this assignment because I was given free rein and could decide on the colors of the table linens, and I'd arrange and rearrange the place settings several times until they were "just right." All the while, Christmas carols played on our radio, and Mother and I sang along with the music. There was great anticipation about the opening of the Christmas presents that evening, and by dinnertime the excitement was at a fever pitch.

My father seemed to know just when to make his entrance. He'd come home a short time before our Christmas feast would begin. A gentleman from the shelter always accompanied him; we learned to expect him but were never certain who it would be. I remember one particular guest who didn't have any shoelaces in his shoes and wore a holey sweater.

No one mentioned this Christmas guest before his arrival, but Mother always prepared more than we could eat, just in case. When Father arrived, he'd smile at my mother and tell her that he'd brought a guest for dinner, then ask for her consent. She'd always appear a little surprised and flustered, but she always answered: "Of course it's all right, Clifford. There's plenty to eat." It took me a long time to figure out that this was just a little game between the two of them, but when I did, I'd secretly smile to myself as I watched their expressions and the sly nuances in their actions throughout the day.

We'd introduce ourselves to our guest, and then sit down to a wonderful feast that Mother had prepared with loving hands. She would hover over all of us, making sure we each had enough on our plates, especially our guest. She had a gift for making him feel a part of our family and not a stranger at all.

I found each guest fascinating and enjoyed talking to him. Following our parents' lead, we shared our lives with him and felt very lucky to have the fine gentleman among us.

Our dinner would be over all too quickly, and then my father would thank the man for coming and enriching our family. Just before escorting our guest back to the mission center, Father would go to the coat closet and say to the man, "It's mighty cold out there, and I noticed you don't have a coat. Here, take mine, and feel the warmth of our family on your journey." The man would gratefully accept the gift, and then Father—dressed in his winter gear but without a coat—would accompany him on the long walk back to the center, which was many miles away.

On his return, we thawed Father out with hot-water bottles before we opened our presents. With great anticipation, Mother always saved her gift for Father until last. He acted surprised every year as he opened up his box to find a beautiful new coat inside.

"I just felt it was time for you to have a new coat, Clifford," my mother would say with a coy little smile on her face. Often there would be tears in my father's eyes; he was usually so touched that he couldn't utter a word. The secret between them would be safe for another year.

As each Christmas celebration came to an end, we stopped and talked about the man who had helped make our Christmas so wonderful. Then Father would get out the Bible and read to us about the first Christmas from the book of Luke:

"And, lo, the angel of the Lord came upon them, and the glory of the Lord shone round about them: and they were sore afraid. And the angel said unto them, 'Fear not: for, behold, I bring you good tidings of great joy, which shall be to all people. For unto you is born this day in the city of David a Savior, which is Christ the Lord. And this *shall* be a sign unto you; Ye shall find the babe wrapped in swaddling clothes, lying in a manger.' And suddenly there was with the angel a multitude of the heavenly host praising God, and saying, 'Glory to God in the highest, and on earth peace, good will toward men'" (Luke 2:9–14).

As I pause to remember that tranquil scene, I can fondly see my mother and father looking at each other with a dear, sweet love in their eyes and a sparkle of the secret they shared that day and would share again for many years to come. My heart will be forever touched by that Christmas coat, by the person who wore it, and especially by those who gave it—my parents—for their lives reflected the selfless love of giving, which is what Christmas is all about.

★

Does the answer to someone else's need hang in your own front closet? Ours is a country of great abundance, as well as desperate poverty and lack. As we buy one new coat after another for various members of our family, and struggle to find more room on the rack, think what a difference donating just one coat could make.

A warm hat, a pair of mittens, and a thick coat will not only protect a needy person on cold winter nights but also allow him or her to literally feel the love and support of their fellow man, and may give them the strength and courage they need to improve their situation once and for all.

The Gift
of Love

A lovely folktale tells us that when Christianity first came to northern Europe, four spirits, or angels, representing different virtues were sent from heaven to place lights on the original Christmas tree. The spirits were called Faith, Hope, Charity, and Love. Their search was long, for they were required to find a tree that was as strong as faith, as high as hope, as sweet as charity, and as everlasting as love.

In the forests of the North, their search ended with the discovery of the fir tree. They lighted it from the radiance of the stars, and it became the first Christmas tree.

Faith, Hope, Charity, and Love—all lofty and noble virtues, but, according to this tale, the only one that is everlasting is Love. Perhaps the angels were right—love transcends time and place like nothing else can. It motivates and inspires and makes us willing—even anxious—to sacrifice for one another. Love is not a single act but a climate, a work in progress in which people learn and grow as their hearts become knit together as one.

They say that "love is in the air" at Christmas—indeed, just by looking at the number of songs and carols written about "the season of love," we know it is so. Christmas magnifies all emotion; love feels sweeter, memories are more poignant, and even sorrow goes deeper. The sights and sounds and smells around us are softer, more magical, more pungent.

If love is a verb, as they say, then it is no more so than at Christmastime, a time when kind thoughts and good intentions are turned into actions. We are more open, more caring, and less likely to ignore the impulse to give of ourselves. At Christmastime, we see signs of love where we didn't notice them before. Consider how one young girl—her pioneer family struggling to survive a hard winter on the plains—recognizes the light of love:

December 25, 1862

All of us children hung up our stockings Christmas Eve. We jumped up early in the morning to see what Santa had brought, but there was not a thing in them. Mother wept bitterly. She went to her box and got a little apple and cut it in little tiny pieces and that was our Christmas. But, I have never forgotten how I loved her dear hands as she was cutting that apple.

—Hannah Dalton Journal

If you want to experience the true miracle of Christmas, give the gift of love abundantly to those you know and love, and even to those you don't.

Christmas Spells Love

CANDY CHAND

"It is good to be children sometimes, and never better than at Christmas, when its mighty Founder was a child himself."

—Charles Dickens

Christmas to a six-year-old is pure magic. Christmastime the year my son Nicholas was in kindergarten was filled with the type of excitement and anticipation you wish would last the whole year through. Santa, presents, cookies, Christmas lights—what more could a child hope for? And this year, he'd be part of the school's winter pageant. His class had been memorizing songs for weeks.

Christmas to the *mother* of a six-year-old is quite another story. Although I had vowed to make the holidays calm and peaceful by cutting back on nonessential obligations, I still found myself exhausted, unable to appreciate the precious family moments and childlike wonder that came so naturally to Nicholas. I made an honest effort to simplify my baking, decorating, card writing, and overspending, and yet I struggled to feel the true meaning and spirit of the season. As I listened to Nicholas practice his songs in the car, I didn't have the heart to tell him I'd be working the night of the big school production.

Unwilling to miss his shining moment, I spoke with his teacher. "Come to the dress rehearsal!" Mrs. Watson said cheerily. She assured me that any parent unable to attend the evening performance would be welcome to come that morning to the final practice. Thankfully, Nicholas seemed happy with the compromise. After all, his mother would see the program before anyone else's mom!

I made an extra effort to arrive a few minutes early that morning, so Nicholas would see me sitting near the front in the school cafeteria. A few other parents quietly slipped in and found seats. Finally, each class, led by their teacher, filed onto the stage and sat down, cross-legged.

As each group stood to perform their song, I thought about the district's policy not to refer to the holidays as "Christmas" and fully expected to hear only the jolly, commercial songs about reindeer, Santa, and snowmen. When Nicholas's class got up to sing "Christmas Love," I was a little surprised—and pleasantly so—by its "politically incorrect" title.

Nicholas and his classmates were aglow, adorned in fuzzy mittens, red sweaters, and bright snowcaps. They wiggled and squirmed like only six-year-olds can, one child gently shoving another into place, another scratching her head through the wool cap. Those in the front and center held up large letters, one by one, to spell out the title of the song.

C-H-R-I-. . . and so on.

"C is for Christmas," they sang, as the "C" was held up high over one little boy's head. "H is for Happy," they wailed, with the same bold confidence as Spanky, Alfalfa, and the gang. And on it went until they had spelled out the complete message, "Christmas Love."

The performance was going smoothly until, suddenly, a few parents began to notice something was wrong. A small, quiet girl in the front row was holding her letter "M" upside down—totally unaware that the letter appeared to be a "W" instead of the "M" in "Christmas." Besides the few adults present that morning, the audience consisted of first- through sixth-graders, who quickly saw the girl's mistake and began snickering and pointing.

But the little child was oblivious. She stood tall, relishing her important role in delivering the song's message, and sang out with all her heart. Although the teachers tried to shush the older children, the laughter continued until the last letter was raised. And then we all saw it together.

A hush came over the audience, and eyes began to widen. In an instant, we all understood the song's new title—and its real message. Parents and children alike saw it—and each one of us, on our own level, suddenly knew the reason we were there to celebrate, the reason for the lights and trees and gifts, the reason for the warm, peaceful feeling in our hearts even amid the excitement and chaos. A few children whispered in reverent tones, others sat with mouths open, pondering the words before them.

The little girl with the "M" card had made a mistake, but her mistake was a gift. I breathed a silent "thank-you" to have been a witness, somehow sensing I'd just been given the great secret to everlasting peace from the hands of an innocent child. For, when the last letter was held up, the message—and the essence of the season—was very clear:

CHRIST WAS LOVE.

And I believe He still is today.

⭐

Candy, the mother in this story, was given a visible reminder of the true meaning of Christmas. Would you like a visible reminder too?

Choose a night during the summer or early fall when you can see lots of stars. Go on a "star trek" with a friend or with your family: drive or climb to a place where you can really see the sky full of stars. Spend some time stargazing or go to an observatory and do the same.

Now think about the star symbol that is used so frequently at Christmastime. What does it represent? Yes, it began with three kings following a bright star in search of a royal birth, but what does it mean to you today? Why do we light candles at Christmas? What does the star light or candle light represent to you?

At home, light some candles and reflect on what brings light to your life. Discuss it with your family. To some it will be the everlasting light of a Savior that seems to shine brightest in their darkest hours. To others it will be a symbol of hope for a better tomorrow—the proverbial light at the end of a tunnel. Ponder the statement "There are two ways of spreading light: to be the candle or the mirror that reflects it" (Edith Wharton) and think of times in your own life in which you have spread light in a small way or a significant way.

Our Pickle-Jar Christmas

Wilma M. Rich

"Every time we love, every time we give, it's Christmas."
—Dale Evans

When I was a child, it seemed to me that Christmastime always began the day Daddy brought home the Christmas tree. But the year I was five, Christmas for our family began much earlier.

Two months before Christmas, on a cold October night, Mama rounded up her six children, including me, and sat us down in the long log room that served as kitchen, living room, and bedroom for the family.

She lifted three-year-old Benny and me onto the high bed with the crazy-patch quilt and gathered the four older children around us.

"Christmas is for surprises," she began. "How would each of you like to make this a special Christmas by surprising Daddy?"

Everyone agreed, and Benny and I squealed and clapped our hands at the prospect of treating Daddy, since he often had special surprises for us in his lunch bucket at the end of a workday.

"Shh! Let's talk quietly so Daddy won't hear. He's just on the other side of the door, remember?" We could hear Daddy hammering and sawing in the new living room he was adding to the room we presently lived in. He was working at home on nights when he worked day shift at the coal mine, and mornings when he worked night shift, trying to finish the room before Christmas so we could have our Christmas tree there.

"You children know how hard Daddy works for us and how he worries about paying the bills?" Mama asked. The Great Depression was drawing to a close, and though we didn't understand that, we did know that times were hard. The older children nodded, and, taking a cue, I nodded too, although I had no idea how much Daddy worked or worried. I didn't even know what a bill was.

Mama bent closer so she could speak quietly and make us all hear. "Since Daddy always makes Christmas so nice for us, I thought it would be fun to make this year Daddy's Christmas." Getting into the spirit of things, we nodded. We loved keeping secrets, especially a Christmas surprise.

"What do you mean, Mama?" asked Sammy, who was two years older than I.

"You may not want to surprise Daddy when you find out what I have in mind," warned Mama.

"Yes, we will!" promised Eva, the eldest and most magnanimous.

Mama continued, "Okay, but you don't have to decide until I explain." She quieted us again, because we were beginning to fidget. "If this is going to be Daddy's Christmas, we'll all have to make a lot of sacrifices." Little Benny's eyes lit up; he loved to make things.

"Number one, none of the rest of us will receive any gifts or give presents to each other." As Mama watched to see everyone's reaction to this bombshell, the room became so still that the sound of Daddy's hammer rang with clarity in the next room.

"No presents?" asked Marilyn and Jerry in unison. I watched Marilyn's tranquil countenance crumble and Jerry's green eyes get bigger, and I began to catch on.

"That's right," said Mama. "Nothing under the tree for any of us except Daddy."

I saw the disappointment among my brothers and sisters, and I would have felt glum too except that I was sure Santa would bring each of us a gift on Christmas Eve.

Mama's lilting voice was gentle with understanding. "Remember the Christmas story? How the wise men traveled many days and nights to bring presents to the baby Jesus?"

I loved all the stories about Christmas and snuggled into Mama's pillow, waiting to hear another one. "Remember the traditional story of the little shepherd boy who heard the angels singing 'Glory to the newborn King' and gathered a tiny lamb to give as a gift to the King in the manger?"

While firelight danced through the holes in the front of our potbellied stove, and Jack Frost painted pictures on the room's north window, Mama retold the story of the wondrous birth of our Savior.

When she finished, she held her arms as though cradling a child. "Jesus, who would someday make the greatest sacrifice of all, meant enough to the wise men for them to give up their greatest treasures to honor him." I was enthralled, as I always was when Mama told this story. I looked at the rapture on the faces of the others and felt tingly inside.

Sammy asked, "Didn't the wise men get any presents when they went back to their houses?"

"No, dear, only a peaceful feeling inside that made them feel happy."

"I don't care about not getting any presents," declared Eva after a moment, her eyes sparkling. The others agreed, although without complete conviction.

Mama studied our faces in the lamp's glow. "Does everyone agree, then?" One by one we nodded. "Are you sure you can all keep a secret?" Several looks were directed at Benny and me. "Will you and Benny promise not to tell Daddy?" Our heads bobbed up and down. "Here's what we're going to do."

As we listened, the chilly October wind whipped leaves against the windows, but we didn't care. Mama could make anything sound good.

The next morning, we started saving money for Daddy's Christmas surprise. Mama made economical foods for the children's school lunches instead of buying small treats to put in them. She let Eva, Marilyn, Jerry, and Sammy put the saved quarters and nickels in a large pickle jar, then we all watched as she placed the jar up inside the tall kitchen cupboard, hidden behind a stack of dishes.

"That's a start," she said. "We'll see how fast it adds up."

And it did add up with each sacrifice we made. Those of us with piggy-banks transferred our pennies to the pickle jar. Instead of buying treats with allowances or spending money when we went to town, we dropped the money into the jar.

Jerry and Sammy milked our black cow, Baby, and turned the handle on the separator while milk whirred into one container and cream into another. Then Eva and Marilyn churned the cream into butter to sell.

One Saturday, Mama took us to the livestock auction in our Model-A Ford truck. We sold our six runt lambs, now grown into fat, woolly sheep. Jerry and Sammy also sold their rabbits, dropping crisp dollar bills into the jar that night.

Each night after school, the bigger kids would hurry home to see how much Daddy had done on the new room, avidly watching the chinked railroad-tie walls go higher and higher. Then we would all help Mama with projects designed to help us earn or save money.

We cut quilt blocks while Mama sewed the blocks together on her treadle machine. We helped her make shirts for the boys from Daddy's old dress shirts, and mittens from old woolen coats. We helped put patches on the knees of jeans, and ruffles on skirts that were too short. My contribution was clipping thread and treadling the machine, when Mama would let me.

Instead of buying new winter coats, Mama handed down what she could to younger ones and made over some old coats she found in a trunk for the others. When the school-age children said they needed new shoes, she asked them if they would rather have new shoes or Daddy's Christmas. Of course, they opted to polish and patch their old shoes and put the money they saved into the pickle jar.

We were enjoying the sight of the greenbacks and coins adding up. Each Saturday evening after our baths in the round metal tub, Mama would take the jar down from the cupboard, and we would count the money.

When the Sears and Roebuck catalog came a few weeks before Christmas, Mama told us we could each choose what we would like and cut the toys from the catalog to give to our paper dolls. Choosing, she pointed out, was as much fun as having.

Benny and I would save the treats Daddy brought home to us and let Mama send the cakes and cookies with him the next day, thereby saving the money she would have spent on more treats for Daddy. She would let us take pennies from her coin purse and drop them into the pickle jar.

November came and went, with Daddy putting up two-by-fours and planks for a roof on the new living room, then covering the boards with a tin roof. He laid the floor in early December and started plastering the walls two weeks before Christmas.

Making Christmas candy was always a special treat. This year, instead of buying sugar, syrup, canned milk, and nuts, we put the money away and made honey candy. While we stretched the hot candy like taffy, we sang Christmas carols.

Daddy worked almost through the night two nights before Christmas, putting the finishing touches on the new room and bringing in a stove for heat. He was eager to present the finished room to us as his Christmas gift to our family.

The next morning, the family—wrapped in quilts with heated rocks at our feet—loaded into Daddy's old truck and chugged through new-fallen snow to Clarks Valley to cut a Christmas tree. We chose a fragrant piñon tree with pinecones still clinging to its branches, and Daddy chopped the tree down while we kids romped in the snow and exchanged secret smiles. All day Daddy quizzed Mama about Christmas gifts for the children, but Mama just smiled and said, "Don't worry, everything has been taken care of."

That night we wrapped Daddy's gift with bright red-and-green paper while Daddy made a stand for the tree. We trooped behind him into the new room as he carried the tree to a corner. In awe, we looked around us. The new living room seemed like a magnificent castle. We decorated the tree with paper chains, popcorn, and our traditional Christmas angel, and then sang Christmas carols and knelt around the tree for a Christmas Eve family prayer.

On Christmas morning, Daddy woke us with a boisterous, "Ho, ho, ho! Merry Christmas! Wake up, sleepyheads, and let's go see what's under the Christmas tree." We rubbed our eyes and smirked and giggled. We knew what was under the tree! Daddy had put a big log in the stove the night before, and this morning the room was toasty warm and smelled of pine and new plaster.

Mama and her brood of little ones hurried into the room ahead of Daddy, all of us thrilled with the new room he had built, and anxious to see his face when he noticed the tree.

"Whoa!" Daddy exclaimed as he studied the empty floor under the tree, empty except for one gaily wrapped package. "Where are the rest of the Christmas presents?"

"Under the tree, dear," replied Mama, her eyes glowing like Christmas lights.

"But I don't understand."

"Just read what's on the tag," instructed Mama, giving him a push.

"Yes, read it, Daddy!" exclaimed Sammy, whose curiosity was getting the best of him. "Read it! Read it! Read it!" shouted the rest of us.

Daddy picked up the gift and read aloud, "To Daddy on *your* Christmas, from all of us with love. Signed, Ellen (Mama), Eva, Marilyn, Jerry, Sammy, Wilma, and Benny."

"Surprise!" we shouted when Daddy took the wrapping from the present. Inside was a box, and inside the box was a neat stack of bills—some for building materials for the new room and some for groceries and utilities, bills that had mounted up during the years of the Depression—each marked "Paid in Full."

As Daddy looked at each paper, his eyes misted over and he hugged and kissed each of us in turn, starting with Mama. "This is the best Christmas I've ever had," he choked through tears.

None of us has forgotten the look on his face that morning, and "Daddy's Christmas" will remain in our hearts as the best Christmas ever for us too.

✳

Working together on a family project brings such a feeling of closeness and satisfaction, at the holidays or any other time of year.

Close your eyes and remember the feeling of perfect peace you have on Christmas morning. Your family is still in their jammies, carols play softly on the stereo, and for once the messy living room strewn with shredded wrapping paper doesn't get on your nerves. Yes, you may be exhausted from assembling toys the night before, but the little annoyances of life fall away and you can focus on what really matters: the love you have for your family, and their love for you.

Now, how can you recreate that feeling more often than just on Christmas morning? Every family will have its own ways, but working together in the garden, cooking a special dinner together in the kitchen, creating a family emblem or flag, or some other project that brings you close for an extended period of time will create bonds of love and long-lasting memories for your family.

You could also try having a once-a-month "Play Hooky Saturday." Clear your calendar ahead of time and plan to spend the whole day doing whatever your family likes doing best. Disregard the chore list, ignore the dishes, don't answer the phone, and forget crossing things off your "to do" list. The only rule is that whatever you choose to do can't cost a lot of money. The time spent "in the present" with your family will strengthen your family's foundation of love.

Letters to Uncle Ed

Marianne Jennings

"The only gift is a portion of thyself."
—Ralph Waldo Emerson

Every year between December 20 and December 24, my children and I feed ducks in the park. We do so because people are busy and the ducks get hungry.

We discovered our ducks quite by accident. I'd promised my children a picnic in the park but had repeatedly put it off. "It's too hot," I kept telling them. This excuse lasted until November. Then I faced the end-of-the-semester crunch with whining and panic on both sides of the desk.

I finally got around to the picnic, courtesy of Taco Bell, on December 20. You don't think of ducks as being Beefy Burrito fans. But in the photos I took of our first "picnic" years ago, you can see a head, an arm in the air with a Taco Bell wrapper, and what appears to be a white-and-orange full-length ball gown. Eager ducks mobbing a child produce something just shy of a Diana Ross concert look.

As I watch those hungry ducks, I think how wonderful it would be if everyone could be as happy about a simple gift. How many times in our lives do we get this kind of reception?

During the duck fiesta, my mind wanders to relatives—and to Uncle Ed. Uncle Ed was my father's half-brother. When he was young, he suffered a head injury in a car accident and was left with "the seizures," as the neighbors used to say. In those days, such a disability was a sentence to isolation and unemployment. He lived with my grandmother and busied himself with high school basketball games, barbershop talk, and yard work.

We visited my grandmother often, and Uncle Ed was a fixture. Sometimes the neighborhood children would tease us about Uncle Ed. But Ed always sat on the porch and watched us play while the other adults enjoyed quiet moments inside. He used to call me "bad boy," both for my energy and for my choice of play activities. He also taught me how to use a hand mower to mow a lawn, and he showed me how to paint a fence.

Uncle Ed had a small income from Social Security. I often heard adults in the family say his money was stashed away because he sure wasn't paying for food. We moved from his small town when I was in high school, but he wrote letters to me, and my father encouraged me to write back. When I did, the letters began, "Dear Uncle

Ed, I am fine. How are you?" They ended two lines later with, "Well, gotta go."

Our correspondence spanned two decades. When I fell short of a prompt reply, he would write again and comment about the delay. When I was attending college in Utah he wrote, "I thought you fell off a mountain." Once I'd moved to Phoenix he wrote, "Did you get lost in a mirage?" I wrote back out of obligation, never more than a page.

Several years ago, Uncle Ed had an extended hospitalization. I called to check on him. He was unable to speak, but the nurses told me they had read him my letters and several columns I'd sent. "We like them" one nurse said.

After a long battle with his illness, Uncle Ed died. My father attended the funeral, but I was nursing a child and didn't go. When he returned, my father said the only personal belongings Uncle Ed left were a tool chest full of tools and a fishing tackle box.

"What was in the fishing box?" I asked him over the phone. "All his money?"

"You'll see when you come to visit," came his mysterious response.

During my next visit home, Father handed me the red tackle box. I sat alone and opened it. There in that box was every letter I had ever written to Uncle Ed.

In that box was my high school graduation picture, the first picture of my firstborn, and every picture of each child since then. There was a wedding picture and announcement. There was a college graduation announcement. There was a small picture my daughter had drawn. There was a picture of us feeding the ducks.

Then my father told me Uncle Ed had taken only one trip in his life. He had come to my wedding reception.

I had no idea that anything I did or said was important to Uncle Ed. But now, as I looked back on twenty years of my life, I wondered why I hadn't said more.

During the holiday season, we all search for the gift that will cause us to be treasured and remembered by the recipient—and for always. Those gifts are with us each day.

As I watch the ducks this year, I'll think of Uncle Ed. And this one last time, I'm writing to him again: "From your bad boy who wishes she had done more. Gotta go."

✯

We seldom get the chance to know what kind of impact we've had on those around us, and when we find out it's often too late. Why not reflect on this more often?

Once a month during the year, give yourself this test before going to bed: If tonight were Christmas Eve and Santa was drawing up his list of naughty and nice based on today's behavior, where would you fall? Be honest, now. If tonight were Christmas Eve and you were headed off to midnight services, would your heart be filled with love? What small changes can you make in your life to be able to feel that kind of peace and love tonight? Tomorrow?

Instead of lying awake tonight thinking about what didn't get done, or worrying about the problems you'll face tomorrow, focus on what was accomplished today and what it might bring to others. Did you give a smile and a kind word to a stranger? Did you give a family member a pat on the back for a job well done? Did you give your full attention to the four-year-old with the skinned knee?

Take inventory of the level of giving and receiving in your life, and go to sleep concentrating on those gifts.

An Angel in Deed

AMANDA ROWE

"How many dormant sympathies does Christmas awaken."
—Charles Dickens

Mommy! We're going to put on a Christmas play!" my five-year-old daughter, Lauren, exclaimed as she jumped into the car after school one day in early December. "And all the parents get to come to it! And we get to wear costumes and everything!" she continued, hardly able to contain herself.

Now that Lauren was in school, I loved hearing the account of her school activities every afternoon when I picked her up. With Christmas approaching, her enthusiasm for the Nativity play was delightful. Each day she would tell me of the various preparations being made for the performance—she'd sing me the songs they were learning and recount the familiar story of the birth of Jesus with childlike wonder.

One afternoon Lauren was especially excited; she announced that she had been chosen to play the part of an angel. She went on to describe the beautiful white dress she would wear and talked happily about the golden tinsel that would adorn her hair. Over the next few days, as the rehearsals became more intense, her excitement continued to grow, so I was slightly puzzled when she arrived home one afternoon and made no mention of the play.

A few days later, Lauren came home and immediately started rummaging through her box of dress-up clothes. I asked what she was looking for, and she told me she needed a dull, plain dress to wear for the school play. Puzzled, I asked about her angel costume.

"Well, Mommy, there's a little boy in my class who doesn't get along very good with the other kids. Nobody likes Charlie very much because he's kinda bad all the time," she explained quietly as she searched for just the right costume.

"But what does that have to do with your part as the angel?" I asked, still confused but somewhat concerned about where this was heading. Lauren explained that this young boy's role in the play was to be part of the crowd of people in Bethlehem, but despite instruction and rehearsal, his constant fidgeting on stage was disruptive. To help keep Charlie quiet, the teacher had asked Lauren to forgo her part as an angel and stand in the crowd scene beside him so he wouldn't disturb the flow of the performance.

"I told the teacher yes," Lauren said, keeping her eyes focused on the box of clothes. "So now I need to find a costume for my new part and one for Charlie too—in case he forgets to bring one."

My indignation rose as I absorbed what she was saying. Why should she give up her special part for a troublesome classmate? As I looked at Lauren, however, I held my tongue and instead commended her for her thoughtfulness. Still, a nagging irritation stayed with me throughout the night.

The next day, I broached the subject with Mrs. Roberts, her teacher. She told me that recently she had watched a relationship develop between Lauren and Charlie. As other children had scorned him and laughed at his clumsy ways, Lauren had begun to befriend him. It seemed that Lauren was helping him through the play and that she had also been assigned to sit next to him in class. I related my concern that, in looking after Charlie, perhaps my daughter would fall behind in her own work and miss some opportunities.

"Oh, Lauren is a very bright little girl," Mrs. Roberts said, smiling. "She gets on with her work quickly and efficiently and then spends time helping Charlie with his tasks while others are finishing," she explained. "Lauren is patient and understanding with him, unlike any of the other children, and his work has improved and his self-confidence has blossomed. By becoming his friend, she has done more for him in three weeks than I, a qualified teacher, have been able to do in three months!"

I left the classroom with a spring in my step. The loving attitude of my five-year-old daughter was humbling. All the way home I wondered whether I, an adult, would have had Lauren's quiet courage and her ability to show love and acceptance to someone who wasn't easy to love.

That evening, as the lights came up on the Nativity play, there was a general stir in the audience as the little angels in white dresses and sparkling tinsel halos came on stage. But one mother, at least, recognized the glowing inner beauty of a little girl in a dull blue dress standing in the middle of the Bethlehem crowd scene—holding tightly onto a little boy's hand.

✫

Lauren put her friend's needs before her own, surprising her mother with her maturity. How is it possible that her mother hadn't noticed this quality in her child before? Children grow and change so quickly—delighting us and challenging us every step of the way. Too often, we neglect to let them know about the times we catch them doing something good.

If you use Christmas stockings in your family, hang them up early—maybe the week before Thanksgiving instead of in December with the rest of your decorations. Then jot down compliments for each person in your family on slips of paper and secretly place the notes in their Christmas stockings throughout December. Focus on positive qualities and acts of love, service, or sharing you observe during the month. Also include notes about things you've noticed in general during the year—improvements they've made, talents they've developed, problems they've solved, times they've made you laugh.

On Christmas Eve, have each family member read the notes in his or her stocking. If you're a family who displays a Nativity scene in your home, you might even have everyone place their notes at the foot of the baby Jesus as you explain that their good qualities and acts of love represent their gifts to the Christ Child.

A Miracle of Love

GEORGE PANNOS

"This is the message of Christmas: We are never alone."
—Taylor Caldwell

This is a true story. It is not about me, but it is about those close to me.

Maria and John grew up together in a small town in Iowa. When she was fifteen, her family moved to another state and they lost touch with one another. They had felt a loving connection since early childhood, and had proclaimed that they would be together forever. But fate had other plans.

On a hot August night in a hospital outside Reno, Nevada, Maria, now forty-five years old, was succumbing to stomach cancer; the doctors had given her only a few days to live. As it happened, John, unaware of the where-abouts and condition of his childhood sweetheart, was visiting an old friend, James, who was recuperating from heart surgery in the same hospital. As John was leaving his friend's room and passing the intensive care unit, someone cut in front of him, causing him to stop abruptly. At that instant, he glanced to his right and saw a woman in an ICU bed—and, because her eyes met his, he smiled and nodded. She managed a smile and slowly nodded back to him.

A strange feeling came over him, and he felt an impulse to approach this woman and speak with her. He stepped into her room, paused, and said awkwardly, "Hi! I saw you from the hallway and just wanted to say hello. I hope you don't mind."

She smiled. "No, I don't mind . . ."

"Are you doing okay?" he asked.

"Sure," she said. "I'm doing okay, and thanks for asking."

They gazed at each other in silence for a long moment. A sacred stillness surrounded the room. Then, to his surprise, he found himself asking, "Do we know each other?"

"You know, I had the same feeling—like we've met," she responded.

"Where are you from?"

"A small town in Iowa you've probably never heard of . . ." Then she saw the look in his eyes, and she knew— against all logic or hope—she knew. "John, is that you?"

"Oh my God! Maria! Tell me I'm dreaming!"

He rushed to her and they embraced tenderly. Maria, with tears in her eyes, held him tightly. "I never thought I'd see you again. You've been on my mind and in my heart for years. Of all the ways I dreamt about how we might meet again, this was *not* one of them."

With eyes full of tears and his heart overflowing with love, John said, "I just can't believe it's you. I never knew how much I missed you till this moment. You never looked more beautiful to me."

Maria began to cry, overwhelmed by joy and sorrow.

For the next few days, they were inseparable. At first the nurses were concerned about John's presence in the intensive care unit, but once their story spread, he became an accepted fixture. After speaking with her doctors, he realized they probably had little time together and that every moment was precious. For Maria and John, time stood still. Their life together was beginning anew.

On Saturday, an extraordinary thing happened: When Maria's doctor came to check her early in the morning, he found her sitting up in bed, smiling and talkative. His first reaction was that, under the circumstances, it was Maria's last hurrah. He'd seen numerous patients who seemed alert and revitalized just before dying. She had already lived beyond the time predicted.

But now Maria's blood pressure, heart, and other vital signs were all normal—the best in weeks.

"Doctor, when can I go home?" she asked.

He smiled and told her he would run some tests the first thing on Monday, and that if they looked good he saw no reason to keep her hospitalized. He felt it was just as well that she die at home in comfortable surroundings, and medically, they'd done all they could.

That afternoon, Maria was moved from intensive care to a room on the top floor with a view of the trees and mountains. John was told that although her signs seemed positive, he should expect the inevitable and to be prepared. John understood, but his thoughts were focused not on the future but on the present. It was all they had.

On Monday, Maria's tests and a scan showed her stomach tumor had shrunk by 20 percent; a second test confirmed the surprising result. Her physician couldn't explain it, but he had seen other spontaneous remissions and said, "I'm guardedly optimistic."

That evening, the pink light of a majestic Sierra sunset embraced Maria and John as they gazed through her window beyond the mountains to the west. The next morning, John called his office in Los Angeles and told them he needed a leave of absence due to a "family matter."

On Tuesday, John took Maria home, where they committed to making up for the lost years in the time they had left together. A month passed—but they hardly noticed the time—and the rose was back in her cheeks. A week later, the doctor found not only that Maria had gained weight but also that the tumor had continued to shrink without chemotherapy. Her eyes sparkled and her hair was growing golden. It seemed they had a new life to look forward to.

Maria and John reminisced about their early years together and became a couple of kids in love again. Each knew what the other was thinking and feeling as if they were one body, one soul.

John resigned from his job in Los Angeles, had his belongings sent to him, and found a new job near Maria that would begin in January. On Thanksgiving Day, their friends celebrated the special day with them. The holiday air was crisp, and a gentle snow began to fall. Maria continued to improve, and the world smiled on them both.

In early December, however, things took a turn for the worse. Maria woke up one morning in extreme pain. John rushed her to the hospital, where she was immediately taken to surgery. But the cancer had spread out of control. The miracle and the dream were ending. Five days later, December 10, Maria went home again for the last time. The doctor gave her some pain medication to be used as needed.

On the way home, they bought a beautiful six-foot Christmas tree and slowly spent hours decorating it at home, savoring every minute. When the lights in the room were dimmed and the tree lights came on, a holy tranquility filled the room. Maria's friend Katie, who came by later, said, "A celestial radiance seemed to grace the house, as though angels were in our midst."

During the next week, friends kept dropping in to visit. Maria asked Katie to pick up a few special presents for John. On Christmas Eve, she and John opened their gifts. The fireplace lit their faces, and in the glow of the firelight, in a timeless foreverness reserved for lovers, their devotion to each other was forged anew. The feeling of

Christmas and the scents of cinnamon, vanilla, and bay-berry filled the air.

Christmas morning was beautiful in its silence. Maria nestled quietly in John's arms. They sipped champagne and made toasts and wished without words.

In the early morning a few days later, Maria reached over and clutched John's arm. He woke up quickly. "Maria, are you okay?"

She answered, her arms encircling him, "Honey, it's time . . . hold me tight!" She looked up into his eyes and whispered, "I don't mind going, but I don't know if I can bear leaving you. Promise you won't forget me . . ."

They kissed. And within a short time, Maria breathed deeply and was gone. On her face was a beautiful smile that spoke of happier days, spring sunshine, love, and eternity. Her face told him she was free from all pain.

Socrates said, "True love comes to pass when one soul occupies two bodies." John knew that one day, a mere blink in eternity, he would rejoin his love. And even though she was gone, she was listening and watching, and her spirit was alive in him.

★

Serendipity. Coincidence. Chance. Fate. John and Maria found each other "accidentally" after being separated for thirty years, and they were able to create new bonds of love before it was too late.

Today, begin an experiment. Operate under the assumption—even if for just one week—that nothing in your life is accidental. Imagine that everyone with whom you come in contact is crossing your path for a reason. Pay attention to your surroundings, to your urges, to your hunches, and write down what you notice. Strike up conversations with those who sit next to you on an airplane or at the doctor's office. Open yourself up to discovering higher meaning in your everyday activities by being receptive and alert.

Express love to those around you during this week, even when you might not be inclined to, and then listen for the various ways love is returned to you. Expect to find miracles, look for divine intervention and assistance in your life, and that guidance will become apparent to you more often than you think.

Aunt Margie's Last Christmas

KIMBERLY RIPLEY

*"I wish we could put up some of the Christmas spirit in jars
and open a jar of it every month."*

—Harlan Miller

Divorce was scandalous back in the 1930s, especially when it was filed by the wife. But Marjorie Tilton was a feisty woman, not one to let society dictate how she should live her life—especially when she knew she had good cause. For the next sixty years, Marjorie worked in a convalescent home, and when she finally retired in her early nineties, she was older than many of the patients living there.

The youngest of nine siblings, "Aunt Margie," as we called her, was my mother-in-law's aunt. She had survived the Great Depression, her own depression, and a world that shunned hardworking, self-sufficient women.

It wasn't until she retired that she started to show signs of aging. We'd get phone calls from the nursing home at seven o'clock at night telling us that she'd shown up for work even though she didn't work there anymore. We'd get calls from the hairdresser saying she had shown up at six o'clock in the evening for an appointment that had been scheduled much earlier in the day. Without the patients she'd cared for in the nursing home for company, she had very little companionship, and we guessed she'd begun to regret that she had never remarried or had children.

Each year we invited Aunt Margie to our home for the holidays, but she had always declined, opting to work on the holiday so that the other nursing-home employees could spend the day with their families. It made her happy to share Thanksgiving and Christmas with the elderly patients, many of whom were forgotten by their own families.

The Christmas after Aunt Margie's retirement, we issued the usual invitation, but we weren't surprised when she declined. I had a hunch, though, that we might just be seeing a little more of her that Christmas, so I planned ahead and tucked away a few extra gifts for her—some gloves, warm slippers, a scarf, and a box of her favorite candy—in addition to the notepaper and stamps she enjoyed receiving every year.

On Christmas morning, my mother-in-law called to say that Aunt Margie had indeed changed her mind. She would like to spend Christmas with us rather than staying home alone in her apartment. I grabbed the extra gifts from the hall closet—each already wrapped and labeled—and simply added them to the family's pile of gifts under the tree.

The children immediately made Aunt Margie feel at home. She watched intently as they opened each gift. She marveled at the dolls my girls received and at the radio-controlled cars the boys were playing with. She had never seen such innovative creations, she said, especially in children's toys. In fact, she was so enthralled watching the children open their gifts that we had to coax her to open hers.

She thanked us quietly for each gift, and tucked each one back in its box, with the wrapping paper neatly folded and enclosed in the box too. She didn't seem particularly excited to receive the presents, and I felt a little hurt that she wasn't more enthusiastic about the thought that had gone into choosing each one. We all guessed that maybe she was simply overwhelmed. After all, it was unusual for Aunt Margie to spend Christmas surrounded by toys and games and clutter and confusion and celebration.

Shortly after the holidays Aunt Margie became ill. After a lengthy hospital stay, it was decided that she needed nursing-home care, and fortunately the nursing home where she'd worked had a room available. When Aunt

Margie had to give up her apartment, my husband and I went over to clean it out. There, stacked neatly in the corner of a room we found each and every Christmas gift we had given her, still in their boxes with the folded wrapping paper inside each gift. She hadn't used any of them.

"Maybe she didn't like them," I said to my husband, Roland.

"She liked them," he assured me. But I wasn't convinced.

As the weeks and months passed, Aunt Margie's health deteriorated. She spent the last few weeks in a hospital, and toward the end she found herself in the company of the pastor of our church. Although not much of a church-goer herself, we always knew Aunt Margie believed. She described herself as an "at-home Baptist," and now, at the end of her life, she seemed to feel at home with our pastor.

"What did you talk about today, Aunt Margie?" we would ask her each day.

"Oh, just the weather," was her standard reply, always accompanied by a sly wink.

Aunt Margie passed away at the age of ninety-three while she was in the hospital, and the same pastor conducted her funeral. He had apparently gotten to know her quite well.

"She loved her work with the elderly folks," he tenderly explained. He described her love of the city where she lived, and the walks she enjoyed taking in her neighborhood. And then he talked about her feelings for children.

But Aunt Margie had never had any children.

I listened more closely.

"She especially loved Kim and Roland's children," he continued. "Watching them play brought her hours of joy. She seemed to lose herself in their childhood fantasies."

Funny. I had never really known how much she enjoyed our children.

"And her very happiest moments," the pastor continued, "came this past Christmas. You see, Margie hadn't spent a Christmas at home since she was a very young girl. And this year she spent it watching the children open their presents and play with their new treasures. She said she felt like a child again herself. She told me it was the happiest Christmas she could remember—being in a warm home surrounded by children and family."

I suddenly understood. I had tried so hard to make Aunt Margie's Christmas a happy one by indulging her with material gifts, when the only gift she truly cared about was being part of our family for the day. Her joy came from watching the children's laughter and excitement and feeling the love that comes from being with family. As it turned out, all the store-bought gifts in the world would never compare to the one thing money *couldn't* buy: belonging and love.

My only regret is that Aunt Margie died without knowing about the wonderful gift she gave our family that Christmas. She gave us something so important that none of us has ever forgotten it: the realization that—at Christmastime, and throughout the year—it is *presence,* not *presents* under the tree, that counts.

☆

Life is fragile, and we never know when one of our loved ones will no longer be with us. Even when an elderly person dies after a long, fruitful life, we sometimes wish we could relive the memories of that person.

As your parents or grandparents get older, be proactive in preserving their memory by making a family-history video. Turn your next family gathering into a fun family documentary, and get the kids involved in producing it too.

This can be accomplished in many different ways, but one simple way is to encourage Grandma, for example, to sit in a comfortable chair surrounded by her family and have her pick questions at random from a hat. These can be questions about her life as a child, her opinions, her favorite things, and so on. If you want to make it even more special, add a slide show of photographs and music from her era to help tell her story.

The format doesn't matter as much as the bonding experience of doing it. Love of family is an integral part of keeping the Christmas spirit alive in your hearts, and preserving memories that otherwise might be lost is one way of generating that love. The finished video will become a treasured Christmas gift to all.

Deciding on Love

SUE PEARSON ATKINSON

"Christmas, children, is not a date. It is a state of mind."
—Mary Ellen Chase

H ow can I tell them we can't afford Christmas?"
Robert asked himself, as he looked at the worried faces of his four young children. They stood
crowded together in the small veterinarian's office, anxiously looking from their father to the vet, and then down
at their quivering puppy. She looked so tiny there on the
examining table. "How can I make them choose between
gifts for themselves and saving the life of a dog?"

Robert and Toni Kerr worked hard to make ends
meet for their family of six—he in construction and she
at the local mail-box store. Without money for lots of
frills, they still tried to provide enough that their children
would not feel totally deprived.

Over the years, Robert and Toni had worked out a
plan to deal with the financial reality of Christmas: it was a

strictly budgeted affair paid for with money set aside each month, starting in January. There would be no annual credit-card splurge for the Kerr family, but with their savings plan they amassed a nice sum of two thousand dollars by December—enough to buy some of the "cool stuff" everyone hoped for, while still living within their means.

This year the kids' requests had been the usual: Hanna whined that each of her friends had a stereo CD player and Walkman; Janelle said she positively could not show up at school without a certain pair of $80 tennis shoes; both Cody and James were begging for a fancy Nintendo set and the games to go with it. All those electronics added up, but Robert and Toni figured they'd still have enough to buy gifts for each other, their extended families, and a few special friends. And, oh, yes, they'd get their dog a bag of rawhide chews to savor. Poof! The money would be gone, but it was certainly enough to serve up a respectable amount of Christmas spirit.

But now their careful financial planning was standing on the brink of disaster—because of a dog. Pawnee, their five-month-old puppy, was in desperate shape at the animal hospital. The possibility that the puppy who had stolen all their hearts might not be around for Christmas brought tears to Robert's eyes. Crowded together in the small room, they all heard the vet's question: Did the Kerrs want to take extraordinary measures to try and save her? Extraordinary measures would add up to a hefty sum—in fact, the entire amount they'd set aside for Christmas.

It had been love at first sight when Robert encountered the puppy months before. He hadn't planned on getting a dog—none of them had—but one day, after picking up young Cody from school, they had dropped in to say hi to Toni at her job and then crossed the street to the pawn shop. His friend Don always set aside tools he thought Robert might want to buy at bargain prices.

"Hi, Don. Got anything for me today?"

"Nothing today, Robert, unless you want a puppy. My dog had a litter, and these little ones are ready to go now." Robert looked into the box behind the counter, and Cody squealed with delight. "Oh, Daddy, can we . . . can we . . . can we?"

Robert picked up one of the fluffy, squirming creatures and held her close to his chest. He had lost his beloved old dog a year ago and vowed he would not get another; the pain of losing such a terrific pal was too difficult. Now this little ball of black-and-white fur had completely relaxed and shimmied up his chest to nestle under his chin. So much for the "never agains," he said to himself. And that was how "Pawnee" came to join the Kerr family, named not for an Indian tribe but for Don's pawn shop.

Toni worried at first that the puppy might not get enough attention from the kids, but she was quickly proved wrong. The girls argued with the boys about whose room and whose bed Pawnee would sleep in each night.

Robert promised his wife that the puppy wouldn't tear up the house when they were all gone for the day, so he took the dog to work with him. He loved having her with him—she was so energetic and quick to learn. In just a few short months he'd taught her to sit and stay, roll over, and lie down. Dogs must be genetically programmed to love riding in trucks, Robert guessed, because Pawnee jumped up and down with pure glee when it was time to head out for a job.

On this December day, Robert planned to finish a retaining wall for a client who lived in the country. When he worked indoors, Pawnee stayed in his truck, but outside work meant she could run and play. Robert knew she wouldn't go far from his side, and if she wandered, his whistle would bring her bounding back.

That day, when it was time to pack up for the day, he called her and she came, but she was walking instead of running. Something was different—on the ride home Robert thought Pawnee was too quiet. As he turned down his street he glanced at the puppy and noticed small bubbles and then foam at the corners of her mouth. He turned the truck around and headed straight for the animal hospital instead of home.

"This puppy is acting like she's been poisoned. Has she gotten into anything?" the vet asked Robert.

"She's been with me all day. We were outside on a job and— oh, no. I'd better call the client." Robert's face was ashen when he reported back to the vet. "Gopher bait. There was gopher bait in the yard."

Hours later the whole Kerr family assembled in the waiting room at the animal hospital. His voice quavering, Robert explained the situation: "The vet doesn't think Pawnee is going to pull through. We can have her put to sleep and save her the suffering, or we can tell them to put Pawnee in intensive care and do everything they can to save her. But the vet says her chance of surviving, even with the medical intervention, is not good."

Hanna looked at Robert with pleading eyes. "But, Daddy, we have to try and save her!"

"Well, here's the thing, kids. If we tell them to pull out all the stops for Pawnee, it will cost about two thousand dollars. That's all the money we have for Christmas. And there's a good chance we could spend all that money and still lose her. As hard as this is, wouldn't it be better to put her down now, save her the suffering, and have money for a nice Christmas?"

Everyone was quiet. Minutes passed. The children held hands and Robert sniffled and blew his nose. Toni looked at the floor.

Janelle broke the silence. "If Pawnee dies, I won't feel much like getting presents."

Cody added his thoughts. "It won't be a merry Christmas without Pawnee, so who cares about the money anyway."

It was unanimous. At home the children said prayers for Pawnee and for the doctors who were now working hard to save her. When they were settled in their beds, Robert and Toni agreed to take turns calling the animal hospital through the night. Neither of them could sleep. At midnight, the staff told them Pawnee's condition was still critical.

Robert called again at 3:00 A.M.

"It doesn't look good. Her vital signs are weakening," the staff reported.

Robert was despondent. This was all his fault. If only he had locked her in the truck. If only they had never brought her home in the first place. Wasn't this the kind of anguish he had wanted to avoid anyway? If only . . . if only . . . if only.

Toni didn't want to make the next call, at 6:00 A.M. She punched in the numbers with a sense of dread. Chewing on the inside of her cheek, she looked across the room at Robert as she listened to the latest report: "Pawnee's breathing is better, and her vitals are getting stronger. I think we've turned the corner." Toni's eyes widened and she sucked in her breath. For the first time in hours she felt a glimmer of hope.

There were lots of tears in the Kerr home that day, but they were not tears of grief. Pawnee even had the strength to lick James when he pressed his face close to hers at the hospital. By the end of the week, the puppy was home again, nestled among small feet in warm beds following the familiar ritual of arguing over who got to sleep with her. Everything was back to normal. Everything, that is, except Christmas.

The bill for Pawnee's care came to $1,960. Toni looked at the figure written on the paper before her. "Robert, the kids ought to have something—anything. Let's give them the $40 left in our Christmas account."

On Christmas Eve, Robert took the children to the Dollar Store with their ten dollars apiece to spend. Toni caught a glimpse of them through the window as they piled out of the car on their return. But what was wrong? It looked like her husband was crying.

"Robert! What is it? Was it awful to see the kids with only ten dollars to spend for Christmas?"

Robert wiped his face with the back of his sleeve, grinning through his tears and shaking his head as he answered. "No, honey. It wasn't awful. It was wonderful.

The children were chattering, giggling, and poking one another as they dumped their loot on the dining-room table. There was a bag of small rubber reptiles, little-girl plastic jewelry, some candy, Old Maid playing cards, and a Star Wars sword that was already broken. One shopping bag still lay on the floor unopened.

Janelle picked it up and dumped the contents on the floor. "We all agreed to spend only five dollars apiece so we'd have twenty dollars to spend on Pawnee's Christmas." Their mother looked at the pile of rawhide chews, a Frisbee, a new collar, dog biscuits, and an assortment of toys for Pawnee, and tears began streaming down her face. She looked up at Robert standing proudly behind his giggling children. "I guess when it comes to love, there's no such thing as sacrifice," he said to his wife.

Hanna stroked Pawnee as the dog excitedly began to poke through her pile of treats. "Daddy, I think this is the best Christmas we've ever had."

"Without a doubt, Hanna. Without a doubt."

★

In searching out the origin of Christmas customs, we are often led back to St. Francis of Assisi, whose love reached out to all of God's creations. He especially advocated showing special consideration and kindness to his friends the animals. There are numerous tales relating how various animals came to worship the Christ Child, and St. Francis wanted to remind us that animals should be treated with the same respect and love we show all living beings, just as the Kerr family did in this story.

"If I could see the emperor," St. Francis often said, "I would implore him to issue a general decree that all people who are able to do so shall throw grain and corn upon the streets, so that on this great [Christmas] feast day the birds might have enough to eat."

Plan a day in the fall or winter (or even on Christmas afternoon) for your family to go outside and give the birds a special treat. Tie bits of food—bread, nuts, berries, strings of popcorn—to the branches of a tree, creating a sort of Christmas tree for the birds and smaller animals. Talk to your children about having reverence for all of God's creations.

Our Twelve-Day Christmas

JANET SEEVER

"Christmas is most truly Christmas when we celebrate it by giving the light of love to those who need it most."

—Ruth Carter Stapleton

Twinkling lights on the Christmas tree reflected off the red, green, and blue ornaments, while candles waited to be lit. Outside, a few snowflakes drifted down as the gray Sunday-afternoon sky darkened. Night comes early in mid-December.

Although it was less than two weeks before Christmas, I found it difficult to be in a festive mood. I went through the motions of putting up a few decorations around the house, but my heart wasn't in it this year.

Our family was going through one of the most difficult years of our lives, with major health concerns, a serious work-related problem for my husband, and difficulties with our teenage son. We were facing decisions in the months ahead that could alter the direction of our lives for years to come.

Yes, Christmas was coming, and I knew I should be focusing on the birth of Christ. I tried to remember God's goodness and blessings, but I found myself distracted and discouraged by the overwhelming challenges we were experiencing.

"Mom, I wish we could spend Christmas with Grandpa and Grandma in Minnesota. I miss them, and all my aunts and uncles and cousins," said Rachel, age fifteen, as she sat on the floor wrapping a small package for one of her friends. A wave of homesickness swept over me. Because of the distance, we had spent far too many Christmases away from our extended family.

"I know you'd like to spend Christmas in Minnesota, Rachel. So would I." I looked up from the notes I was writing on my printed Christmas letters. "But Minnesota is twelve hundred miles from Calgary. You remember how hard it was to drive in that snowstorm two years ago? And then the temperature dropped to thirty degrees below zero on the way back."

"I remember. Tim and I almost froze our feet when the car heater stopped working."

We had concluded that driving home for Christmas was simply too risky and that buying airplane tickets for four people was financially out of the question. No one would be coming to our house for Christmas either; I just didn't have the energy to invite anyone. We would be spending Christmas alone.

My thoughts were jolted back to the present when the doorbell rang. "Rachel, will you please get the door?"

As she opened the door, her voice registered surprise. "Mom, there's a box with presents on the doorstep . . . and nobody is out here!" I walked to the door and helped her bring in the box. Who could've left it?

The box contained numerous packages wrapped in bright Christmas paper. Each had a typewritten tag: Open December 15, Open December 16. There were a total of twelve, for the "Twelve Days of Christmas." The first day, December 14, was attached to a turkey wrapped in plastic so we wouldn't miss the fact that it needed to go right into the freezer and not under the tree!

The next tag read: "Our love is given anonymously, so enjoy this with your family, but don't tell anyone, please!" Now we were really mystified. Curious but grateful, I put the turkey in the freezer and the rest of the gifts under the tree.

For the next eleven days, we'd gather together as a family, read the clever little note inside that day's tag, and then try to guess what the package contained. It became a game for us, and even our teenage son joined in on the fun. As the days slipped by, we discovered white potatoes, sweet potatoes, a package of marshmallows, cranberries, packages of gelatin, pickles, olives, cans of green beans, corn, mints, ginger ale, and nuts. Together the packages made up a complete Christmas dinner for four people.

Each time we opened a package, we realized someone was thinking of us, loving us, wishing us a wonderful Christmas. We felt cared for by someone—and that someone wished to remain anonymous.

As it turned out, a few days before Christmas a family from work invited us to join them for Christmas dinner, so we celebrated New Year's Day with the goodies our benefactor had thoughtfully given us. It took the sting out of being unable to go home for the holidays. We felt truly blessed, and so thankful to be loved.

In the following years, the Lord helped us unravel the knot of difficulties one by one, and many were interrelated. The life-altering decision never had to be made, health concerns were diagnosed and treated, a solution was found for the work-related problem, and our son outgrew his rebelliousness. Now, four years later, our nightmare year seems like a distant memory. We have healed as a family.

Did we ever find out who provided the anonymous Christmas gifts? No, we never did. At first I wanted to know—to be able to thank them—but soon it became unimportant. Eventually, I realized that knowing would spoil the experience. The gift had been given out of love with no strings attached. We'd done nothing to deserve it and could do nothing to pay back what they had given us. The gift came when we needed to be reminded most that someone cared. I still have the little tags folded in a page of my journal, and the memory tucked away in my heart.

Our "Twelve Days of Christmas" was a symbol of God's gift to us at Christmas—a Holy Babe in a manger. The gift was given with no strings attached, something that was neither earned nor deserved. Love freely given with no thought of return? That's what Christmas is all about.

Perhaps, as with God's love, the only way to say "thank you" is to pass it on.

★

A simple tag with the words "Our love is given anonymously" made all the difference to one family who was feeling lonely at Christmastime. The written word has incredible power—power to heal, to comfort, to express feelings that might be difficult to express face-to-face. A written card or note might be the very thing to bring a smile, or to lift someone's spirits at a critical moment in their life.

This year, make a point of sending cards or notes to friends and loved ones for no special reason. Hide "love notes" around your house from time to time to express appreciation for your children, and make a game of looking for them. Write a love letter to your spouse and give it to him or her on a random day of the week. Leave notes in lunches, on bathroom mirrors, tucked in suitcases when someone is trav-

eling, or in tennis shoes before your son's big basketball game. Write a note of appreciation to someone at work who went out of their way for you. Write a thank-you note to your child's teacher for their day-after-day dedication.

There are many reasons to express appreciation at times during the year other than birthdays, weddings, and holidays. See how many times you can bring sunshine to someone's life simply by writing a note.

At Christmastime—and always—look a little deeper into your heart to find the gifts only you can give—the gifts of Faith, of Hope, of Charity, and of Love.

CREDITS